URBAN DESIGN MADE BY HUMANS
A Handbook of Design Ideas

Anirban Adhya and Philip D. Plowright

Routledge
Taylor & Francis Group

NEW YORK AND LONDON

Cover image: Anirban Adhya

First published 2023
by Routledge
605 Third Avenue, New York, NY 10158

and by Routledge
4 Park Square, Milton Park, Abingdon, Oxon, OX14 4RN

Routledge is an imprint of the Taylor & Francis Group, an informa business

Library of Congress Cataloging-in-Publication Data
A catalog record for this book has been requested

ISBN: 978-1-032-18517-0 (hbk)
ISBN: 978-1-032-18519-4 (pbk)
ISBN: 978-1-003-25493-5 (ebk)

DOI: 10.4324/9781003254935

Typeset in Myriad Pro
by Apex CoVantage, LLC

URBAN DESIGN MADE BY HUMANS

The design of urban environments is complex and involves diverse needs, organisations, professions, authorities, and communities. It requires relationships to be constructed and sustained between infrastructure, resources, and populations across multiple scales. This can be quite daunting. However, at the core of urban design is a simple idea—our urban spaces are designed to allow people and communities to thrive. For that reason, a good starting point for urban designers is to focus on the way people think when engaging our built environment. This thinking is embodied, developed through the interactions between our mind, body, and the environment around us. These embodied concepts are central to how we see the world, how we move and gather, and how we interact with others. They are also the same ideas we use to design our environments and cities.

Urban Design Made by Humans is a reference book that presents 56 concepts, notions, ideas, and agreements fundamental to the design and interpretation of our human settlements. The ideas here parallel those found in *Making Architecture Through Being Human* but extends them into urban environments. *Urban Design Made by Humans* distinctly highlights priorities in urban design in how we produce meaningful environments catering to wider groups of people. Each idea is isolated for clarity with short and concise definitions, examples, and illustrations. They are organised in five sections of increasing complexity. Taken as a whole, the entries frame the priorities and values of urban design while also being instances of a larger system of human thinking.

CONTENTS

What This Book Is About

WHAT THIS BOOK IS ABOUT

DOI: 10.4324/9781003254935-1

THIS IS A BOOK OF IDEAS that we encounter in cities. These ideas have a particular relationship and effect on how we think and design our urban environments through urban design. Urban design can be considered from many different points of view and involves many different people from architects, landscape architects, planners, and engineers to residents, investors, policymakers, and politicians. In this book, we consider urban design as the experience of our physical environment in the relationship between massing, infrastructure, and habitation that spans the scale of a city block to a metropolitan boundary. Massing means all the physical objects in an urban area, such as buildings, signs, and street furniture. Infrastructure is the underlying support that makes a city work from roads, sewers (grey infrastructure), public transit, power delivery systems, water (blue infrastructure) and natural environment resources (green infrastructure). Both massing and infrastructure affects, and is affected by, habitation patterns. Habitation is people. It is how they live which, ultimately, is why the city exists.

This book is meant as a resource for individuals learning about urban design, but it also presents a shared language of concepts to improve cross-disciplinary and interdisciplinary work. Since urban design involves so many different disciplines and practices, defining some common terms enables us to agree on what is important in urban experiences. Some of the entries in this book parallel those found in *Making Architecture Through Being Human*, the companion book for architecture. Like *Making Architecture*, this book highlights the role of human senses and mobility in the design of our environments. However, the content in this book is engaged at the scale of the city and urban life.

THINKING IS DESIGNING

THIS BOOK STARTS WITH a simple premise—the act of design is not making objects or producing drawings. These are simply the tools we use to explore and understand the intentions of a project. Rather, design is the thinking process that is behind those outcomes. We use our design tools, whether models, maps, diagrams, renderings, animations, and so on, to develop ideas, document intentions, illustrate outcomes, and communicate these things that do not yet exist to other people. The design aspect is about making decisions, managing information, setting priorities, and integrating these into larger relationships.

The second premise of the book is that the thinking process we use in design is based on fundamental human thinking that is embodied. Embodied thinking is the idea that we understand ourselves and the world we live in through a shared relationship between a mind indivisible from our senses and a body situated within an environment. This relationship is a feedback loop that starts with our bodily experiences structuring our thinking, and our thinking then influencing the interpretation of our bodies through actions in its environment. We begin with physical experiences of movement and seeing to understand more abstract experiences such as value judgements, impressions, social interactions, and belief systems. We can find many examples of these physical-to-abstract mappings in the words we use, such as *giving* people ideas as if they were objects, considering process as *forward* as if it was spatially located, or describing things that seem smart as *bright* or aspirational as *lofty* or *up*.

More importantly for us as designers, we use the same embodied concepts to interpret the environment around us and make it sensible for ourselves. Consider how an object at the end of a perceived axis or at a centre is interpreted as more important than other objects around it or attracts more of our attention. Or, when several things are clustered

DOI: 10.4324/9781003254935-2

together, we give them an implicit relationship. None of these things are real in the sense that they occur outside of human judgement. Spatial hierarchy, for example, is something that people decide rather than something that is decided for us. While many of these embodied ideas might seem simple, the simple ideas are fundamental to understanding more complex ideas in our environment.

The ideas found in this book are scaleless and ahistorical. We, as humans, use them all the time to understand and engage in many things. However, when we restrict our thinking to urban design, these ideas have a particular effect at a particular scale and take on nuances of meaning that exist only within the context of a city. While there are many other complex and important aspects of urban space, such as social differences, belief systems, varying cultural rituals, and diversity, the basis of humanness comes from our capabilities of perception and action as we move through the city and experience it. We build these basic ideas into understanding social relationships through proximity, visibility, and similarity. We inherently look for patterns and organising principles that allow us to quickly interpret our surroundings, making us more successful at navigating complex urban environments. They also define a set of priorities for urban design, which offers an underlying framework to define urban design as a discipline and highlights a common core to engage urban design principles.

URBAN DESIGN IS NOT BIG ARCHITECTURE

WE OFTEN THINK ABOUT cities as simply being the result of a collection of buildings. As such, it is natural to consider the way we design cities and the way we design buildings as being the same thing, even going as far as to think about a city as a type of big house. In fact, before the early twentieth century, architecture and urbanism were taught, learned, and practised as inseparable acts. The first professional urban designers were simply architects applying their skills to the city instead of a building. However, is urban design simply architectural design with more buildings in a larger area? Or, more precisely, does the design of a single building, the focus of architecture, and the design of a collection of buildings, the focus of urban design, use the same values, ideas, and skills?

The purpose of urban design is the development of cities as a human settlement, which could be considered a very old activity. However, urban design is relatively new as a theoretical and professional discipline and is still rather ill-defined. One of the issues in defining urban design is that so many people are involved in the development of cities in so many different ways. As there are many competing priorities in agreeing how a whole bunch of people should live and act together, the result is a definition of urban design that includes different priorities and points of view. This can be vague and confusing, as designing for large amounts of people at multiple scales and including many different events lead to issues with diverse objectives for different populations. To introduce a little clarity, we can examine the two words present in the term 'urban design'. Starting with the second word, *design* means that we are concerned with determining a future condition that does not yet exist. To do this, we use the type of information that people already know and that has relevance in our lives. This

DOI: 10.4324/9781003254935-3

starts with the embodied knowledge that develops through the relationship between our senses and our environment. Scale matters in this. The *urban* part of the term highlights human action—a type of information focused on people in how we reside and move at larger densities. It also includes human relationships as a type of information focused on how we interact with other people, how we create rules, rituals, and order, and how we organise our environment for use by people. This understands urban not necessarily to be a city as an object but as the gathering of multiple layers of human activity in a finite space.

This book presents a point of view that suggests that while urban design is based on the same embodied knowledge as all formal design disciplines, it develops that knowledge in a specific way which is aligned with the success of its particular purpose. As explored in this book, urban design concepts have a different focus from that of architectural concepts. Urban design does share interest in the orientation and massing of buildings. However, the change in scale between the individual building and the massing of multiple buildings in a settlement introduces many other factors and voices. Urban design expands the focus from the architectural objects to the infrastructure systems and their human experience. The change in scale of urban design introduces concepts that do not exist in architecture as well as similar concepts that are not applied in the same way.

HOW TO USE THIS BOOK

THIS BOOK IS INTENDED to be a resource of ideas that are based on ourselves and the way we understand the world around us. These also happen to be the same ideas we use to design a world that people can understand. The ideas are simple and based on fundamental human thinking yet are typically not explicit and often ignored. They are so simple, in fact, that we forget that they matter. While many of the ideas in this book are found in all aspects of human life and at many different scales, within these pages they are defined for the context of urban design. While the book uses physical examples found in our urban environment, the point of the book is to illustrate the cognitive aspect of those examples as part of our human thinking structure. Much of the content of this book might be things taken for granted by an established urban designer. However, for someone new to the discipline, this book will provide clear access to ideas, processes, and terminology which are at the core of an urban design practice.

The model of the book is a dictionary or glossary which presents each idea as simply and clearly as possible. This is done to make the information more accessible and legible. The entries should not be interpreted as being absolute or a fixed set of rules by which to design cities. Rather, the book is simply meant to bring awareness to a type of information that is useful if we believe our built environment has a direct relationship with the people who live in it. The content presented here is foundational and advisory. These concepts are persistent aspects of human interpretation of urban environments, but we hardly ever experience them as isolated occurrences. Since they are situated and always found in a context, no entry should be considered as a discrete instance. The principles and concepts should be assembled, arranged, explored, and tested through your own practice.

DOI: 10.4324/9781003254935-4

As a glossary, this book is not intended to be read from cover to cover like a novel or chapter by chapter like a textbook. The entries are divided into sections as a way to increase accessibility and are based on increasing complexity. The first section presents a series of fundamental embodied concepts that form the basis of human thinking. The second section extends these ideas into more specific urban situations. The third section builds from the first two to address spatialised human social interactions. The final section then considers how shared human agreements interact with the ideas presented in the first three sections.

Within the sections, entries are simply arranged alphabetically. This is done to suppress interpretation of any larger hierarchical or epistemological relationship by the order of entries where none exists. *Balance* is before *Grain* simply because 'b' is before 'g' in the alphabet. In this way, the book should be understood as systematic rather than linear. While one person might start at the beginning and read through the entries in order, another reader might simply turn to an entry that is relevant to something they are thinking about. They might then follow related ideas either forward or backwards in the book as each entry is linked to other related entries. This is done through references found in brackets within the text. There are two types of reference. The first uses the format of '(see *Reference*)' and refers to entries in this book. The second reference is '(see *MATBH: Reference*)' and refers to entries in the previous book *Making Architecture Through Being Human*. While *Making Architecture* focused on architectural examples, some of the entries describe the relations between objects (i.e., buildings) which is relevant to urban design. These references are there to remind readers that each entry is part of a larger system of meaning.

FORMAL
CONCEPTS

DOI: 10.4324/9781003254935-5

CITIES ARE EXPERIENCED THROUGH human movement and occupation. When we move through a city or inhabit a place, the basis of our understanding comes from the embodied knowledge gained through sensory experiences of our bodies in a particular physical environment. The core of these embodied concepts is based on human actions of movement and gathering, on human understanding of axiality and containment, and on human interactions with others through density across different boundaries. This knowledge is used to bring order to our surroundings and organise our understanding to build more complex ideas of navigation, publicness, and coherence.

Urban design operates at a scale much larger than the human body, but we use the basic capacities of our bodies to make and understand that design. Our individual experiences of movement and containment is the basis of understanding cities as a large interconnected system of shared experiences. Movement involves notions of generators (where we start), attractors (where we want to go), habitation patterns, daily needs, and formal ordering principles. These help us understand how interrelated resources might be accessed or how a larger territory can be coherent by extending the pattern of a smaller fragment. The idea of containment extends into concepts of edge, boundary, enclosure, extension, compression, and expansion. Motion and containment are, in turn, associated with the core urban concept of human density. The entries in this section address these basic concepts. Their importance is not as isolated ideas but as a foundation for more complex notions, ideas, and actions in constructing environments.

AXIS

AN AXIS IS AN IMAGINARY LINE that we draw in space. We associate this line with an object or a void by thinking about it as defining the centre of mass of something. The axis then extends through or from that point. In this way, an axis is a tool we use to understand our environment through identifying primary relationships based on location, extension, measure, and intersection.

The idea of the axis starts with our body and how we engage the world. Our body is directional, as we know ourselves to have a front and back, left and right sides, as well as a top and bottom (see *MATBH: Orientation*). The position of our major sense organs—our eyes, nose, and mouth—on one side of our body creates the idea of front (see *MATBH: Front*). Our joints, hands, and feet are all articulated to have a primary direction. When we think about moving forward, we extend a line into space to project where our body will go. When we gaze forward, we think about our sight being a set of rays extending from our eyes to connect with things around us. Rays are straight lines that pass through the same point—in this case, ourselves. The projection of ourselves into the environment through extending an imaginary line from our bodies is the beginning of understanding axis (see *MATBH: Relationship*).

While an axis is imaginary, it is very useful as we use this idea to help us understand and bring order to space. The Cartesian coordinate system associates one axis with each of the three major dimensions of length (x), width (y), and height (z). These are the basic building blocks of understanding human environments. In urban design, the prevalent use of the axis is related to voids connected to the experiences of movement and visibility. Extending our bodily experiences to open space, an urban axis is the main line of direction, motion, growth, and expansion in the city. It also controls the activities and infrastructure supporting urban

DOI: 10.4324/9781003254935-6

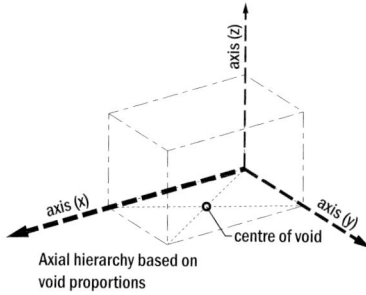

axis (z)

axis (x)

axis (y)

centre of void

Axial hierarchy based on
void proportions

SPATIAL DEFINITION through axis

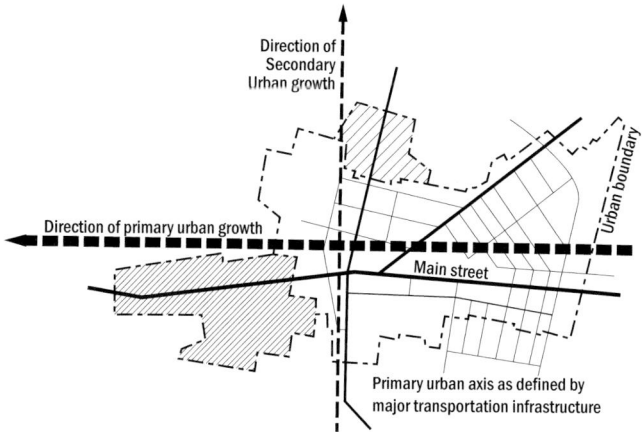

Direction of
Secondary
Urban growth

Urban boundary

Direction of primary urban growth

Main street

Primary urban axis as defined by
major transportation infrastructure

URBAN axis

development. A strong or prominent axis is characterised by long vistas and often terminated by socially important buildings, monuments, or public spaces. An urban axis might also have strongly defined edges or a combination of more or less defined terminations and edges.

As part of ordering systems, an axis is one of the ways we make the world sensible to humans. A single axis defines a void prioritising two events or objects at the ends. A relationship is created between these two urban moments through the imaginary line we draw between them. The quality of this axial relationship is expressed through characteristics of movement and visual perception along the path. The introduction of presence at the end of an axis implies movement along the axis through a sense of destination (see *Path* and *Landmark*). It also orientates our attention to that point and makes it important. When we have two axes crossing each other either at a right, obtuse, or acute angle, we have an intersection. Rather than drawing attention to an endpoint, it is the point where two axes intersect that becomes the site of attention, as they imply a centre point. An axis added to a centre can imply movement as part of a radial system (see *Centre*) or can indicate the connection between nodes (see *Node*). Finally, when we have at least two sets of perpendicular axes, we have a grid (see *Grid*). The starting point for all of these ordering systems is the axis as a line in space.

monument

building

Axis by strong TERMINATIONS

park

Axis by TERMINATION and EDGE

Axis by LINEAR PROJECTION and EDGES

Axis by EDGES

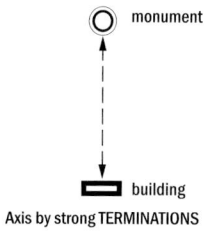

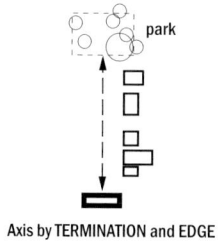

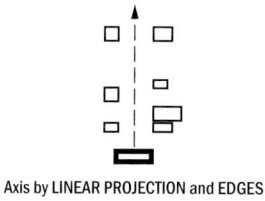

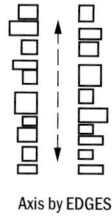

Axis through PRESENCE and EDGE

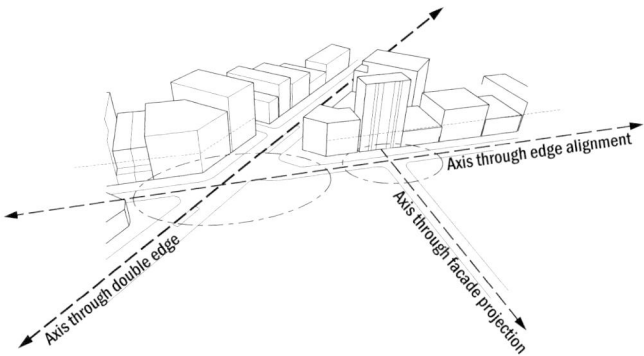

Axis through edge alignment

Axis through double edge

Axis through facade projection

ATTENTION through AXIAL INTERSECTION

BALANCE

BALANCE IS OUR EXPERIENCE of our body's relation to gravity—or at least, that is where it starts. We live in an environment in which we need to maintain some equilibrium or we will fall over. This equilibrium, our sense of balance, allows us to stand up, to understand up from down as well as other orientations; it is the basis of our ability to move and at the core of how we engage with our world. However, while balance starts with our body as an internal physical sense, people commonly use the physical experience of balance to understand things that are not physical—primarily visual information or abstract ideas. In both cases, we use balance to interpret spatial organisation through relating individual parts to each other and how they form a whole.

We understand balance in two primary ways—through either symmetrical or asymmetrical relationships. Symmetry creates static balance by mirroring relationships of elements on two sides of a perceived axis (see *Axis*), where both sides carry the same sense of weight through similarity (see *MATBH: Similarity*). We interpret things that are symmetrical as being very stable, unchanging, and with little to no implied motion (see *MATBH: Implied Motion*). This implies calmness, steadiness, and durability which, culturally, associates symmetry with tradition and universal order. Asymmetry, on the other hand, is dynamic balance that implies motion, action, engagement, and competition between dissimilar design elements. These elements are given equal visual or conceptual weight through creating similar importance. For example, a small object will be less prominent than a large object, but if it is moved further away from the implied axis and coloured brightly, it will be understood as having the similar visual weight as a large, dull object closer to the implied axis. Asymmetry is culturally associated with action, excitement, and change.

DOI: 10.4324/9781003254935-7

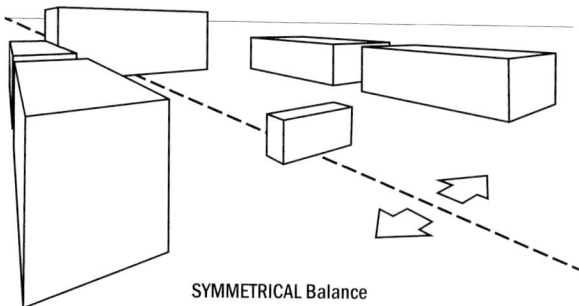

SYMMETRICAL Balance

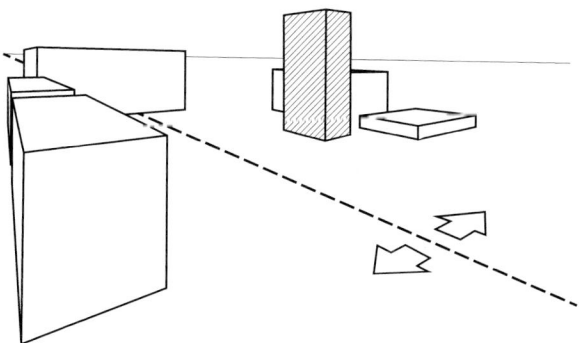

ASYMMETRICAL Balance

FORMAL Balance

Visual balance is based on how we give objects in our field of view a perceived weight and relate them to each other. For urban design, the objects in our field of view are usually the arrangement of buildings in a street-wall or an urban scene. The type of information we use to understand visual balance is based on the shapes, materials, colours, textures, and size of physical objects in the environment, such as buildings or roads, parks, street furniture, signs, bollards, lights, and so on.

A more complex and abstract understanding of balance in urban design is based on performative experience or how we perceive our environment through interactions. When we engage a space for different groups of people which allows for equitable choices by all, we consider these spaces to be socially balanced. This goes beyond visual interpretation and engages abstract ideas such as privacy and publicness, land use, mobility, and accessibility. Experiential balance might also be symmetrical, with the same choice available to everyone, or asymmetrical, where choices are equitable but not equal—which means everyone is provided something but not the same thing. For example, a balanced approach to open space access in a community does not necessarily mean exactly equal amounts of private garden space for every household. Experiential balance for access to open space might lead to larger private gardens for higher-income households and, on the other hand, shared backyards and community gardens for households with lower economic capacity.

Our interpretation of balance is essential to make sense of our urban experiences. Balance helps us in organisation, coherence, and legibility of urban elements as well as in judgement of their spatial use.

Public park

URBAN BLOCKS WITH EQUAL ACCESS TO COMMUNAL GREEN SPACE

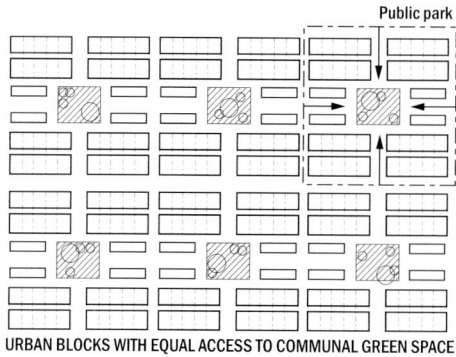

EQUAL (symmetrical)

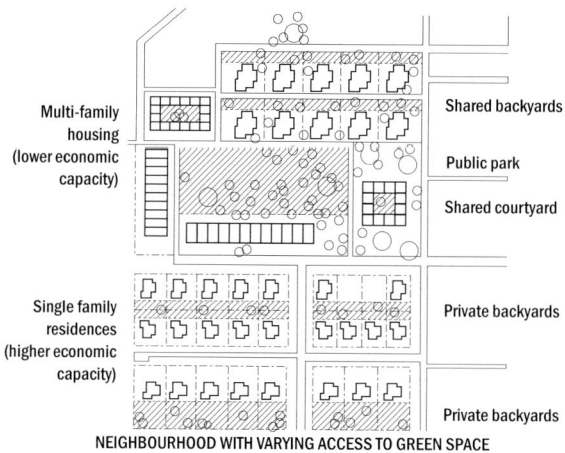

Multi-family housing (lower economic capacity)

Shared backyards

Public park

Shared courtyard

Single family residences (higher economic capacity)

Private backyards

Private backyards

NEIGHBOURHOOD WITH VARYING ACCESS TO GREEN SPACE

EQUITABLE (asymmetrical)

PERFORMATIVE Balance

BOUNDARY

A BOUNDARY IS A SERIES of connected edges that creates a separation between an object and something else. The object can be physical or imaginary, but, regardless, the boundary encloses an area at the furthest limit of that thing. The presence of a boundary suggests insides and outsides connected to the extra concepts of empty and full as well as entering and exiting (see *Containment*). While a boundary creates a discrete entity, it is also a site of engagement that negotiates the relationship between what is inside and what is outside. Everything within the boundary is expected to have a shared relationship. Everything outside is expected to be different from, or not related to, what is on the other side of the boundary. Once we have insides and outsides, we can use a boundary to classify, group, and organise objects or spaces.

In urban design, boundaries are containers and enclose large volumes of space through different types of edges (see *Edge*). These edges are often imagined through legal agreements, present through massing or physical elements, or emerge through lived experience and social interaction. A boundary affects urban design decisions through influencing where and how we build or what we wish to control. It influences urban massing and grain (see *Grain*), types of materials used and their stylistic representation (see *Identity*), and types of uses we consider to be appropriate or would like to encourage (see *Use*). A border is a specific type of boundary between political jurisdictions such as nations, townships, or urban districts. This boundary is imaginary, created through human legal agreement, and affects the nature of the built environment through codes, laws, attitudes, and policies. That boundary might be imaginary in that it exists on a legal document like a zoning plan; but it will also be perceived through the physical effect of those agreements on scale, massing, grain,

DOI: 10.4324/9781003254935-8

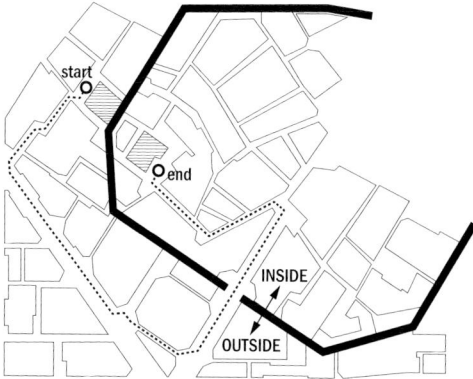

Strong boundary supporting separation
(restricts mobility infrastructure)

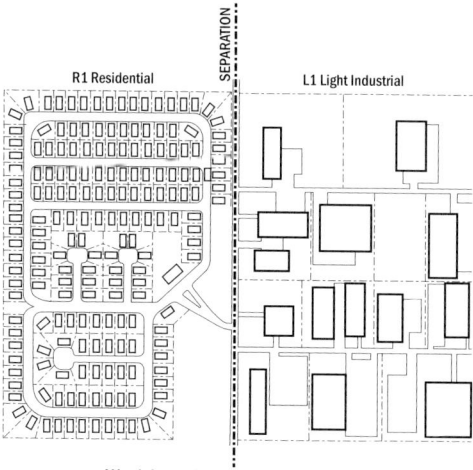

Weak boundary supporting separation
(affects building grain, massing, and mobility infrastructure)

Boundary and SEPARATION

and materiality of the buildings within one bounded area when compared to another.

Boundaries can be strong or weak as well as support interaction or reinforce separation. The nature of the boundary is based on urban massing, infrastructure (transportation, sanitation, communication, resource access), and allowable usage. A strong boundary separates through a physical edge which limits or controls movement. This edge might be expressed physically through massing like in a historic walled city. The edge might also create a strong, separated boundary through control of movement, such as in a contemporary gated community. A weak boundary would be border markers or zoning land division such as a shift between residential and light industrial land use.

A bounded area can look inwards to reinforce its identity over the relationship between that contained space and the adjacent areas (see *District* and *Identity*). Boundaries might also look outwards and activate the adjacent areas. An urban district focused on restaurants and retail could push its massing, activity, and public land use to the edges of its contained area, often leaving the centre to residential, recreational, and more private occupancies. However, if the restaurant district pushed its activities and massing to the centre of the spatial volume, the edges would be used to support connections through transportation infrastructures. The boundary would be used to connect the central activities to other spaces of the city which would be population sources outside of the boundary. In both cases, the events of gathering, eating, and other socialisations would be supported through building grain, plot size, road width, and the distribution of mobility infrastructure.

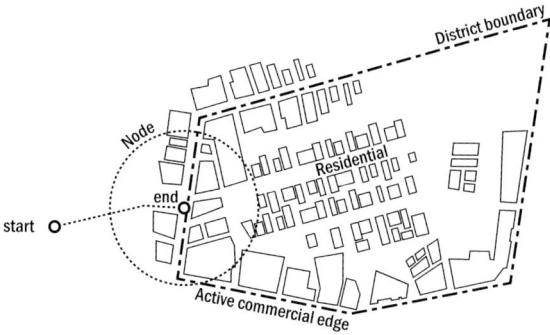

Strong boundary supporting edge interaction
(affects building grain, massing and mobility infrastructure)

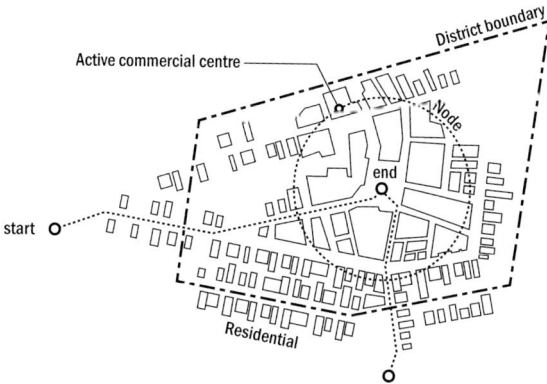

Weak boundary supporting centre interaction
(affects mobility infrastructure)

Boundary and INTERACTION

CENTRE

A CENTRE IS A SPECIAL LOCATION IN SPACE understood as a point equidistant from all edges of a perceived boundary. The idea of centre starts with our body and the extension of our senses outwards into the world around us. Our body is a centre from which our senses extend outwards. The closer something is to our body, the more influence and control we think that we have over it because we can touch it or interact with it in some way. However, when something gets farther away, we perceive less and less control until finally we mark a boundary where that thing is beyond our control (see *Control*). That boundary is known as the periphery. The periphery is considered to be the farthest point where the centre still has influence. We use this embodied knowledge to organise and understand other physical and abstract experiences. We expect that being closer to a centre means something is more important, has more influence, or should have attention. Being further away suggests the opposite—less importance, less influence, and less attention. Once past a periphery, we understand that there is no longer a relationship between anything outside of the boundary and the centre. The influence of the centre is often understood as a ray or an axis radiating outwards from a central point.

In urban design, centre is a spatial ordering principle that operates at multiple scales and can be found in conjunction with other ordering principles (see *Axis*, *Grid*, and *Node*). The basic application of centre is through the introduction of a focal point into an urban development pattern. That focal point needs to radiate presence in many directions. This is often characterised by a core which has either field or axial visibility through height, a surrounding void which defines its periphery or radiating axial voids (see *Corridor*, *Figure-Ground*, *Visibility*, and *Presence*). Strong centres have compact, dense cores (see *Density*). They are marked by significant urban objects like historic buildings or monuments, public events

DOI: 10.4324/9781003254935-9

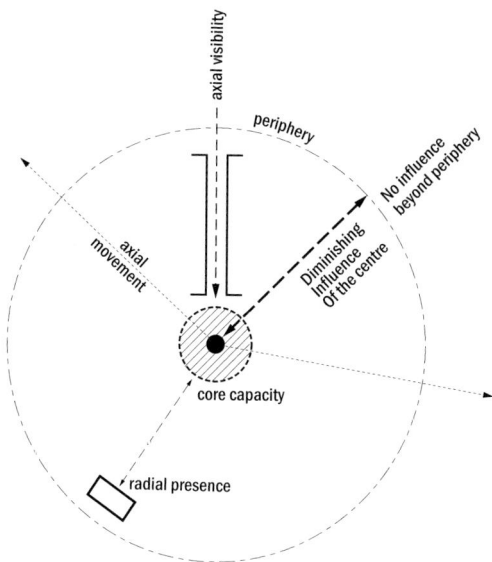

CORE-PERIPHERY relationship in centre based on
AXIAL VISIBILITY and MOVEMENT

like a public plaza or park, and infrastructures like fountains or a municipal facility. At block and district scales, a centre is often associated with two or more axial lines such as streets or boulevards that provide access to the core through movement (see *Path*). At a city and metropolitan scale, the relationship between a densely populated urban core and the less dense surrounding territories, such as suburbs or satellite towns, is an example of a centre-periphery structure.

Centre is also a social idea related to population densities—it is an area where the most activity takes place, as well as a point of engagement, activation, and density (see *Activation*). As a social concept, centre is characterised by two elements: threshold and range. Threshold is the minimum critical mass of population or density required to generate a sense of attraction and gathering around a centre (see *Capacity* and *Accessibility*). Range is the marking of a periphery and is the maximum distance to which the effect or attraction of the centre is perceived. For example, if we consider a neighbourhood, the neighbourhood centre is often composed of common resources like a school and infrastructure such as a community park. For this centre to be effective and functional, we need a certain number of residents within the physical boundaries of the neighbourhood as a minimum threshold. The centre also has a range defined by the maximum distance that residents of the neighbourhood are willing to travel to access its centralised resources.

implied centre

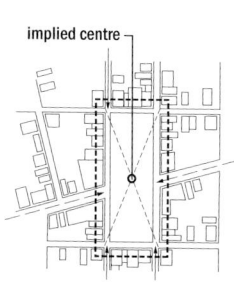

Block scale
(urban void - weak centre, strong edge)

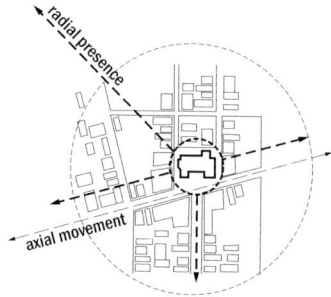

radial presence

axial movement

Block scale
(urban solid - strong centre, weak edge)

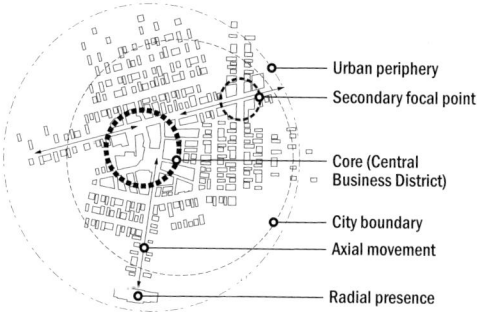

Urban periphery

Secondary focal point

Core (Central Business District)

City boundary

Axial movement

Radial presence

City scale

Urban periphery

Edge city

Suburb with weak core

direction of growth axis

Urban core

Satellite city

Satellite town With strong core

Satellite town With weak core

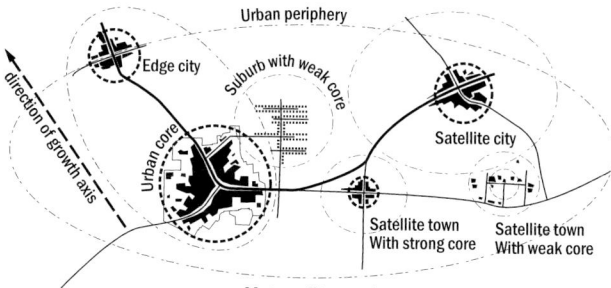

Metropolitan scale

Centre at multiple URBAN SCALES

COMPACTNESS

COMPACTNESS IS A SENSE OF THINGS being close together. It is a spatial idea created when a space is understood as finite while objects and entities in that space are as close to each other as they can be without interfering with their performance. The simplest expression of a finite space is one that is enclosed and has a clear boundary (see *Boundary*). While we might think about compactness as a physical description, it is also a social and experiential idea. When we experience a compact space, it produces different interactions, movement patterns, and relationships compared to non-compact spaces. Compact spaces tend to have higher convexity (see *MATBH: Convexity*), which allow for more socially interactive spaces. These spaces create more opportunities for people to be in the direct presence of other people (see *Co-Presence*) and for people to be aware of other people in the same space (see *Co-Awareness*). The minimum distance found between objects and events in compact space has the effect of increasing accessibility and density.

Compactness typically has a strong part-to-whole relationship which is consistent regardless of the scale in which it is found. In other words, the same qualities of compactness are found across multiple scales of the urban environment from the region (extra-large), city (large), neighbourhood (medium), and block (small). In all these cases, compactness is present through clear boundaries, strong enclosure, close proximity, and an increase in density of objects (i.e., buildings), activities, and people. This generally results in a low void–to–built form ratio, which simply means there is less open space when compared to buildings in areas that are compact (see *Figure-Ground*). A compact city, for example, has clear boundaries and limits development outside of those boundaries to increase the internal concentration of objects and activities within the city (see *Density*). This creates a strong and clear distinction between the city

DOI: 10.4324/9781003254935-10

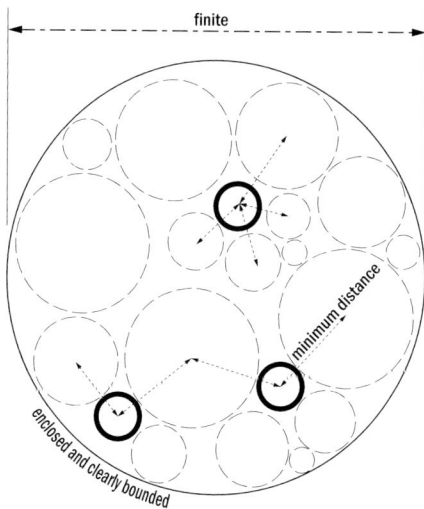

Compactness in relation to SIZE and BOUNDARY

from its surroundings. Highly compact small towns are similar with a well-defined development boundary surrounded by rural open space.

Compactness creates spaces that are highly accessible and efficient. This means that more resources are easily available within a closer proximity. A compact city, for example, is characterised by a larger number of people residing in a specific area (high residential density). Distances between people and resources are short where people can comfortably walk from one place of activity to another (see *Walkability*), or different events and functions in the city are integrated together in a limited area (mixed land use). This decreases travel time between people and needs. Because of this, compact space is often characterised by efficient movement infrastructure such as a transit system, path, or road network. It also usually involves diverse resources in a small area through mixed-use development. A public square with high compactness will have multiple choices of mobility through the space and a large range of possible activities in a small area from sitting, eating, playing, working, and conversing. Likewise, a compact neighbourhood will have a well-defined boundary, low open space-to-building ratio, and different occupancy types mixed together including residential, commercial, institutional, and retail with short paths of travel between these. Across these scales, a compact city will allow for easy movement from a residential alley (walking) to a neighbourhood street bus stop (local bus service) to a city metro station (commuter rail) to a regional transit hub (high-speed rail). At the same time, each area will provide a wide range of access to resources and needs within a small area.

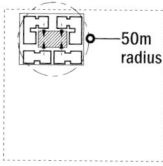

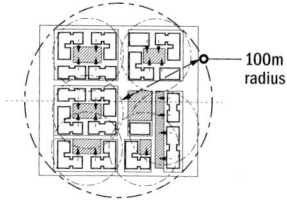

LOT and BLOCK level
(built form – open space ratio)
(pedestrian movement)

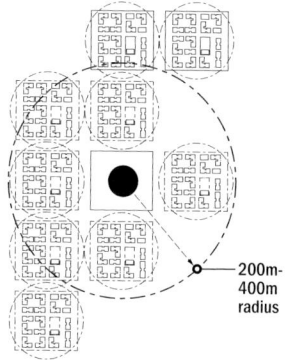

50m radius

100m radius

NEIGHBOURHOOD level with BLOCKS
(hierarchy of open space)
(slow collector streets)

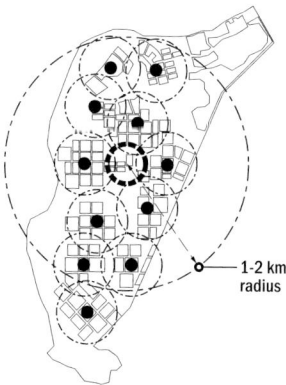

200m-400m radius

TOWN/CITY level with NEIGHBOURHOODS
(green space network)
(medium to high speed arterial roads)

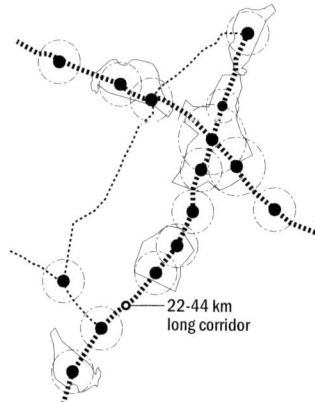

1-2 km radius

REGIONAL level with TOWNS
(corridors and growth boundaries)
(high speed movement networks)

22-44 km long corridor

Compactness at NESTED SCALES

COMPLEXITY

COMPLEXITY DESCRIBES HOW PARTS MAKE a whole and how a whole becomes more than the sum of its parts. It is an organisational state where different elements interact with one another at multiple scales in a structured but non-obvious way. Non-obvious means that complex objects, organisms, situations, and environments involve multiple levels of hierarchy (see *MATBH: Hierarchy*), have low interpretability, and react in unexpected ways. We find complex systems are hard to understand and are often surprised by their outcomes.

Complexity is a human interpretation of the world around us. It is based on our ability to think in terms of pieces and their arrangement in larger and layered assemblages and systems. This experience starts with a series of basic embodied concepts including notions of addition, subtraction, collection, iteration, layering, merger, repetition, splitting, stacking, and linkages. Ultimately, complexity is about the density of information found in an environment that then translates into a particular quality of experience.

Cities are large networks of layered and interconnected environments. In urban environments, complexity involves the relationship among what types of activities and events co-exist (see *Accessibility, Publicness*, and *Use*); how the environment is organised through human perception (see *Legibility, Rhythm*, and *Visibility*); what underlying spatial patterns are present (see *Density, Grain*, and *Diversity*); how all elements interact across multiple scales (see *Connectedness* and *Coherence*); and how urban events and human needs might overlap and change over time (see *Compactness* and *Activation*). Complexity in urban design introduces liveability as well as promotes adaptability, resilience, and interest through diversity to sustain rich experiences for humans.

DOI: 10.4324/9781003254935-11

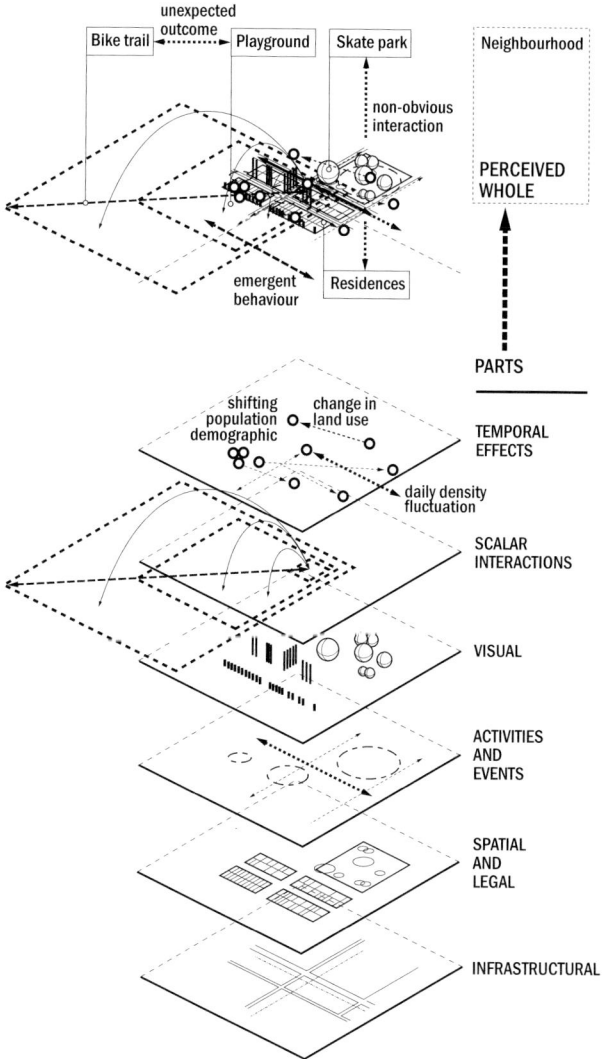

Bike trail → Playground   Skate park   Neighbourhood

unexpected outcome

non-obvious interaction

PERCEIVED WHOLE

emergent behaviour   Residences

PARTS

shifting population demographic   change in land use

TEMPORAL EFFECTS

daily density fluctuation

SCALAR INTERACTIONS

VISUAL

ACTIVITIES AND EVENTS

SPATIAL AND LEGAL

INFRASTRUCTURAL

MULTIPLE DIMENSIONS of a complex environment

CONTAINMENT

A CONTAINER IS A SPECIAL TYPE of object that can hold something. It has an inside, an outside, and a separation between the two. Our body is the first container that we experience, as we understand that our skin defines our physical boundary and separates ourselves from things around us. Through this, we know that a container is a way to collect things together and keep them safe or organised. We can do the same with other types of matter that would be difficult to handle or might be dangerous, such as liquids or gases. The container is used to protect, limit the effects, or resist the expansion of what is inside from what is outside. Since we know that we can put things into and out of a container, our understanding also includes concepts of entrance and exit, open and closed, full or empty, boundary, edge, surface, and content.

While our knowledge of containment starts with physical experiences, we use the same knowledge for abstractions such as events, phenomena, states, ideas, organisations, and territories. In urban design, any type of information that can be spatialised with a perceived boundary suggesting an inside and an outside is understood as a container (see *Boundary*). Zoning regulations, urban growth boundaries, legal property descriptions, and urban green space allotments are examples of abstract ideas which divide space into containers. Each of these ideas affect the development of urban space inside the container by requiring, encouraging, allowing, or disallowing certain activities, uses, and physical structures.

We use containers to create a relationship between the elements inside the container through their alignment with the perceived purpose of the container. If we draw an imaginary boundary around a space, we naturally associate everything within that boundary together through an act of coherence (see *Coherence*). This helps us organise our understanding of the spaces we live in. If we bound a space to define a greenway, it

DOI: 10.4324/9781003254935-12

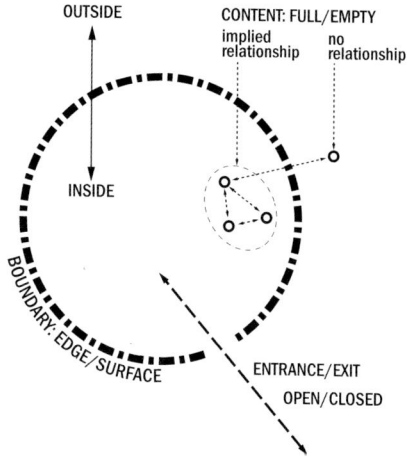

OUTSIDE

INSIDE

CONTENT: FULL/EMPTY

implied
relationship

no
relationship

BOUNDARY: EDGE/SURFACE

ENTRANCE/EXIT

OPEN/CLOSED

Containment based on EXCLUSION and INCLUSION

produces a relationship between the green elements such as trees and wetlands, circulation infrastructure such as paths and trails, the expected use of the space, and the pattern of grain, massing, and development we would allow within the boundary.

Containment can also produce separation. We consider the spaces defined by two containers, or the space inside rather than outside a container, to be different from each other. While a greenway can create a relationship between the elements inside its boundary, we also understand the greenway to be a different and separate type of space to the area outside of its boundaries. The difference is useful in helping us restrict the influence of adjacent areas such as the encroachment of commercial development. The stronger the container concept, the more successful that space can affect separation, isolation, definition, protection, or limitation in the relationship between the inside and the outside. However, sometimes we benefit from weak containers, as by giving up influence or control, we find another benefit such as higher permeability or increased edge activation (see *Permeability* and *Activation*).

Containment can be found at multiple scales, as well as in overlapping and nested conditions. If an object is in a container and that container is in a second container, then we understand that the object is in the second container as well as the first. The interaction between containers allows us to understand a neighbourhood within a district as part of a city having multiple zoning boundaries, nested public spaces such as a square or park with an overlapping transit corridor, all at the same time.

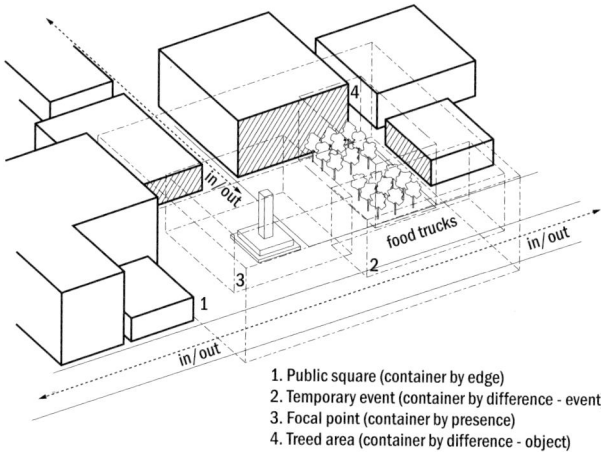

1. Public square (container by edge)
2. Temporary event (container by difference - event)
3. Focal point (container by presence)
4. Treed area (container by difference - object)

Containment with COHERENCE and DIFFERENCE

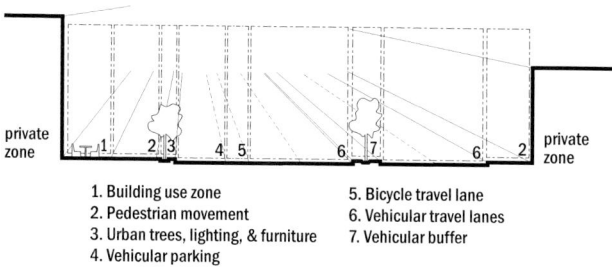

private zone

private zone

1. Building use zone
2. Pedestrian movement
3. Urban trees, lighting, & furniture
4. Vehicular parking

5. Bicycle travel lane
6. Vehicular travel lanes
7. Vehicular buffer

Containment at STREET SECTION

DENSITY

DENSITY IS A DESCRIPTION OF how close or far away elements are from each other within a defined space. It is a measure of compactness. In order to have density, we first need to be able to identify discrete elements that are bounded or gathered around a point (see *Centre* and *Containment*). As density is a ratio between mass and volume, it depends not on the size and shape of the volume or the total number of elements, but on the relationship between the two. For example, we can have a small town and a large city with the same density, or a small town with a higher density than a city.

In urban design, density describes the presence of things in a specific area (see *Co-Presence*). This usually refers to concentration of people (population density), buildings and physical development (massing density), and activities and use (event density). Density is directly related to the richness of urban experiences and quality of life in cities. When we have a higher density, things are closer and more accessible, which increases opportunities for interaction (see *Compactness* and *Accessibility*). An increase in elements possibly encountering each other by being closer and more numerous leads to a more activated space (see *Activation*). A higher density space supports the development of urban infrastructure for movement, recreation, public health, and shared use of resources (see *Connectedness* and *Mobility*). Contrarily, lower density is related to higher social separation, which can be a positive factor for maintaining privacy and individual property ownership.

The consideration of appropriate density is important to develop and support different values of urban experiences as a critical factor in resilient and sustainable settlements (see *Publicness*, *Resilience*, and *Diversity*).

DOI: 10.4324/9781003254935-13

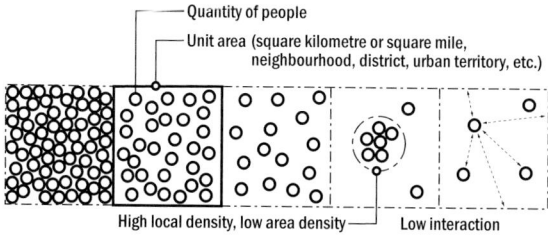

Quantity of people

Unit area (square kilometre or square mile, neighbourhood, district, urban territory, etc.)

High local density, low area density — Low interaction

HIGH ←- - - - - - relationship between people and area - - - - - - → LOW

POPULATION density

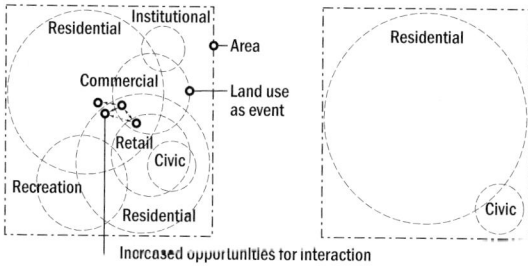

Residential
Institutional
Area
Commercial
Land use as event
Retail
Civic
Recreation
Residential
Residential
Civic

Increased opportunities for interaction

HIGH ←- - - - - - relationship between activity and area - - - - - - → LOW

EVENT density

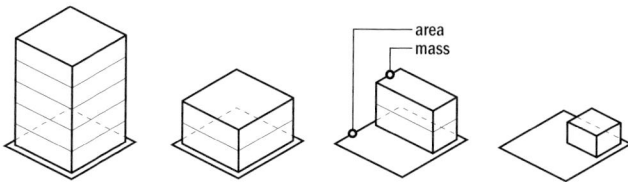

area
mass

HIGH ←- - - - - - relationship between mass and area - - - - - - → LOW

MASSING density

EDGE

AN EDGE IS A PLACE where something stops being itself and becomes something else. It is the outside limit of a thing that still maintains its identity. We find the concept an essential aspect of a boundary where multiple edges are linked together to enclose a space (see *Boundary* and *Containment*) as well as in the identification of a periphery as the edge of a centre (see *Centre*). An edge is an interface as a line of separation, transition, and engagement between two sides of different qualities or identities, such as one passive and the other active, or one private and the other public.

Urban edges can be strong or weak, and activated or passive as well as permeable or impermeable (see *Permeability*) depending on the massing organisation, activity support and movement opportunities. Strong urban edges are created through continuous massing density that aligns with an adjacent void—often a street or public space (see *Density*). Activated edges operate through integrating massing density to adjacent activities on that edge (see *Activation*). Permeable edges relate to how people can move and see when engaged in activities on and across an edge condition. Permeable edges introduce many choices of path and visibility (see *Permeability* and *Accessibility*).

Edges are found at multiple scales. A facade is the massing edge of a building, while each side of the property line is the conceptual and legal edge. Facades of several buildings form a street-wall which is an edge of a block aligned to circulation. Irrespective of the scale, an edge defines the relationships between two territories of space and plays an active role in the organisation of massing and open spaces.

DOI: 10.4324/9781003254935-14

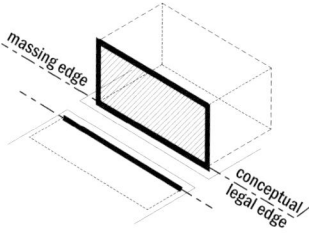

STRONG edge
(continuous massing density)

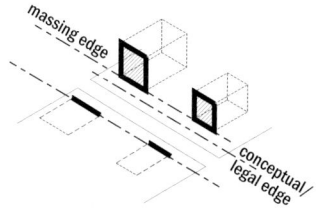

WEAK edge
(broken massing density)

Types of edges based on MASSING ORGANIZATION

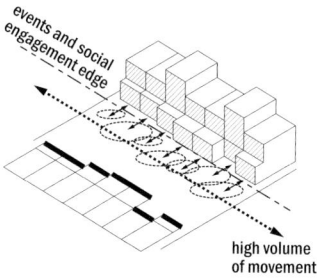

ACTIVE edge
(higher event density)

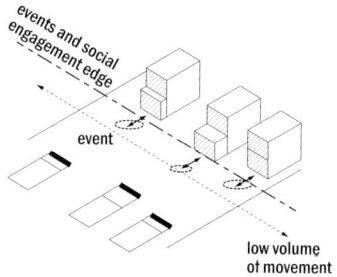

PASSIVE edge
(lower event density)

Types of edges based on ACTIVITY SUPPORT

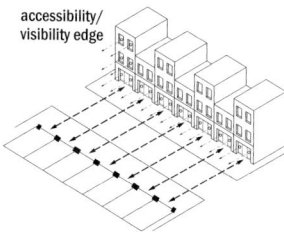

ACCESSIBLE edge
(higher permeability)

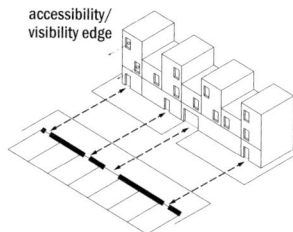

INACCESSIBLE edge
(lower permeability)

Types of edges based on PERMEABILITY

EXPANSION

HUMANS UNDERSTAND EXPANSION as growth connected to health and flourishing—necessary conditions for us to live and thrive. As people mature, we expect to get larger through an increase in height, weight, and size. We see other organisms do this as well, from mammals to plants, insects, birds, and fish. In all cases, expansion is related to increased complexity and associated with life and growth. Contraction, in turn, is related to concepts of ageing, decay, breaking down, and death. In this way, expansion is considered as positive, healthy, and necessary, while contraction is negative and to be avoided. We often leave these concepts unexamined. While expansion is often positive, it can also be negative in certain situations as contraction can be sometimes beneficial and necessary. The important aspects of expansion and contraction are their impact on concentration of people, activities, and infrastructure (see *Density*) and the relationship to availability of more opportunities for more people (see *Accessibility*).

In urban design, expansion occurs to increase the capacity of an environment, such as to accommodate population growth, access cheaper lands, or enhance privacy. As a physical urban event, expansion is based on two major planes—either horizontal or vertical. Horizontal expansion is urban development spreading into adjacent land, usually along existing movement infrastructure. Vertical expansion is the increase of density within an existing boundary through adding vertical mass of taller and denser buildings. Both horizontal and vertical expansion can be symmetrical or asymmetrical as well as axial or radial (see *Axis* and *Centre*). Axial expansion is development that occurs primarily along the line of major transportation infrastructure, while radial expansion extends an area outward from a centre or core. The relationship between expansion and density is a critical factor in urban design. Horizontal expansion is associated

DOI: 10.4324/9781003254935-15

Symmetrical

Asymmetrical

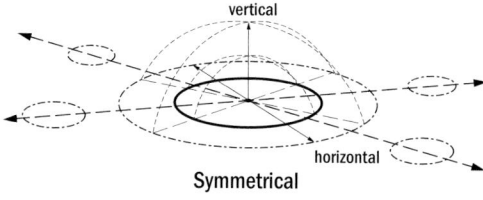

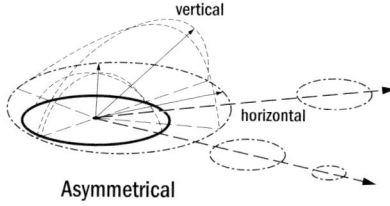

RADIAL expansion

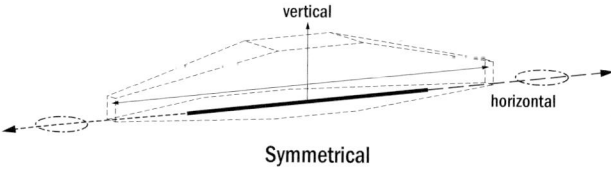

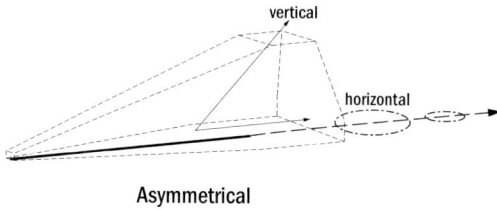

Symmetrical

Asymmetrical

AXIAL expansion

with dispersion of activities and reduction in density. Planned horizontal expansion generally develops along a primary or secondary urban axis or follows major mobility infrastructure (see *Axis*). Unplanned horizontal urban growth often results in *sprawl* or *leapfrog* development. Sprawl is low-density development which is commonly single use and reliant on personal rather than public movement infrastructure, such as residential suburbs. Leapfrog development occurs when undeveloped land is left empty between existing and new development. Vertical expansion, on the other hand, leads to increased density through the concentration of activities, centralisation, and closer adjacencies (see *Compactness*). It can also decrease access to sunlight, affect air movement, and create unequal access to services. Urban development can balance vertical expansion with liveability and environmental quality by using development controls like height restrictions and zoning regulations. Vertical expansion is often associated with a growth boundary, which is a regional boundary that restricts horizontal expansion as a response to sprawl (see *Boundary* and *Density*). As such, any increase in density within an area must be either through urban infill or vertical expansion.

Though growth and expansion are fundamental premises of urban development, there are situations where contraction and scale reduction are necessary due to depopulation and urban deterioration. This is known as shrinkage as an urban principle. Shrinking requires scaling down of infrastructure and the consolidation of massing and activities. Strategically selected areas, such as nodes with enough population density and activities (see *Node*), are selected to remain viable. Other areas are abandoned or have reduced infrastructure, massing, and opportunities of access and activities.

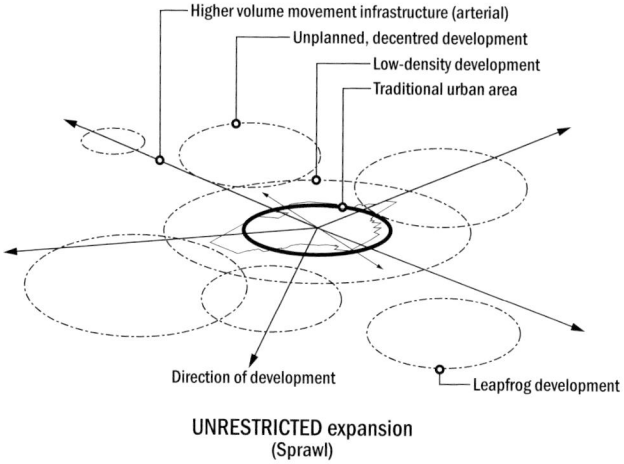

Higher volume movement infrastructure (arterial)

Unplanned, decentred development

Low-density development

Traditional urban area

Direction of development

Leapfrog development

UNRESTRICTED expansion
(Sprawl)

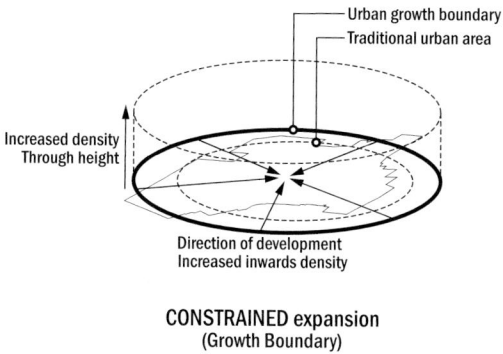

Urban growth boundary

Traditional urban area

Increased density
Through height

Direction of development
Increased inwards density

CONSTRAINED expansion
(Growth Boundary)

FIGURE-GROUND

PEOPLE UNDERSTAND THE WORLD through objects that exist in space. When one of those objects has a noticeable form, outline, or shape, we call it a *figure*. Figures are distinct and discrete from their surroundings. We also expect figures to be contained and individually significant. The space where the figure is located is called *ground*. We tend to prioritise figure over ground because we are aligned to pay attention to objects, so ground becomes *background* or unconsidered (see *MATBH: Object-Ground*). However, both figure and ground are equally important, and neither can exist without the other. While we identify figures through focusing on edges and outlines, it is the ground where we live and interact with others.

In urban design, figure and ground are used as a simplification of the built environment focusing on only two types of information—built masses defined by their exterior edges (figure) and the open space between those masses (ground). Although the figure stresses outline, it is also understood as a solid mass, while ground is understood as volumetric void or 'empty space'. Figure is the part of the environment we cannot enter freely, and one that we experience through its edges as the outer limits of that thing's identity (see *Boundary*). The ground is the part of the environment in which we can move freely with few restrictions. Due to this, ground is also perceived as shared or public space within a city (see *Publicness*).

Figure-ground is a mass-void relationship and important at multiple scales. When the concept is applied to a single building, we define an object and its relationship to its surrounding space. In case of streets and multiple buildings, the relationship expresses the presence or lack of presence of a street-wall as an interface between building massing and supported activities in front of and adjacent to the buildings on the street (see *Frontage*). For a square or a plaza, the figure-ground

DOI: 10.4324/9781003254935-16

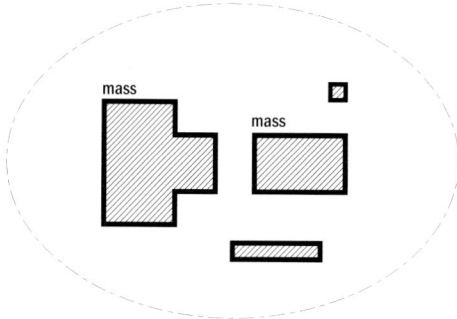

Defined masses (figures) in surrounding void (ground)

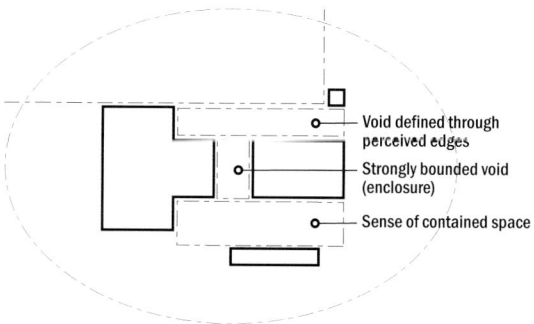

Void defined through perceived edges

Strongly bounded void (enclosure)

Sense of contained space

Void as an object of experience

Figure-Ground RELATIONSHIPS

relationship produces a sense of enclosure and containment, where the void of the plaza is defined by the masses and their perceived boundaries (see *Containment*). The concept is organisational, as it defines access and movement across edges (see *Permeability*), creates identity through strong and weak edges (see *Edge*), and engages these edges with activities and activated frontages (see *Activation*). The figure-ground relationship also allows us to see possible spatial impact, public-private relationships and lived experiences through different patterns of street layout, its granularity, and how activities are concentrated in locations (see *Density*, *Grain*, and *Grid*). This can be connected to the performance of urban developments, as ground is the location for access to natural elements such as light and air as well as visual access in terms of field and axial visibility (see *Visibility*).

While figure-ground might seem simple, the concept can hold quite a bit of social information through human experiences, such as how close someone might live next to someone else, or how visible one area is from another. As such, it is not the individual figures that are important, but their arrangement within a larger ground. It is important in urban design to understand figure in the same way as ground, as a continuous and connected fabric of elements rather than as isolated and individual objects. If either figure or ground is considered as a fragment, it leads to compartmentalisation undermining coherent experience and legibility in urban environments (see *Legibility* and *Coherence*).

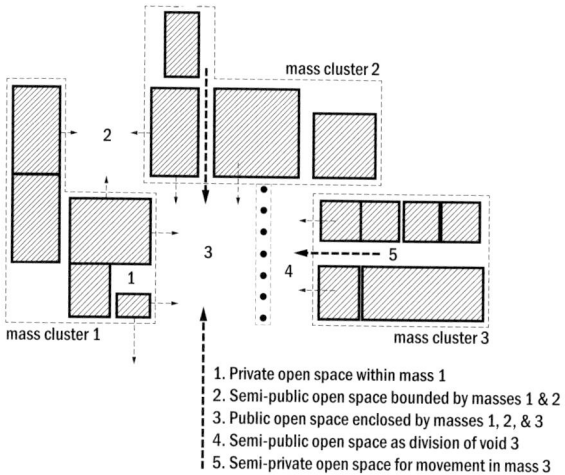

1. Private open space within mass 1
2. Semi-public open space bounded by masses 1 & 2
3. Public open space enclosed by masses 1, 2, & 3
4. Semi-public open space as division of void 3
5. Semi-private open space for movement in mass 3

MASS-VOID configuration supporting different types of social exchange/publicness

Important buildings (mass) and associated open spaces (void):
1 - Municipal building   2 - Courthouse
3 - Religious building   4 - Museum

MASS-VOID relationship highlighting social and spatial hierarchy

Figure-Ground as SOCIAL INFORMATION

GRAIN

GRAIN IS A DESCRIPTION OF the number of elements in a bounded area, how they are arranged, and their scale. The concept implies that the parts make a perceived whole or object where grain is an understanding of how the elements relate to one another within that whole. The quality of the grain is called *granularity*, or the level of detail available in an area or surface based on the amount of elements present. The more and smaller the elements, the finer or smoother the grain and the higher the granularity. Few, large elements in an area create coarse or rough grain. Since grain is not just the amount and size of elements but also their arrangement, grain has configuration and directionality (see *MATBH: Directionality*).

In urban design, grain describes the essential structure of an urban area. This is based on the repetition of a fundamental recognisable unit or seed to create a larger massing pattern that organises the urban environment (see *Pattern* and *Rhythm*). It expresses how land is divided and developed in a built area, usually at the block or district scale (see *Block* and *District*). Grain describes only the relationship of building footprints to open space and the pattern and scale of movement infrastructure such as streets, paths, lanes, and rails. It affects social interactions through movement, accessibility, choice, and interaction opportunities.

Grain directionality is based on the ratio of block length to width. As blocks move towards squareness with equal length and width, the opportunity for access and movement around the block becomes equal. When blocks become longer, there are more opportunities for movement, interaction, and exposure on the short ends as opposed to the long faces. Path options decrease between long blocks which reduces accessibility through lower permeability (see *Path*, *Permeability*, and *Accessibility*).

While urban grain varies greatly from city to city, the basic characteristics are aligned with principles of fine grain or coarse grain as determined

DOI: 10.4324/9781003254935-17

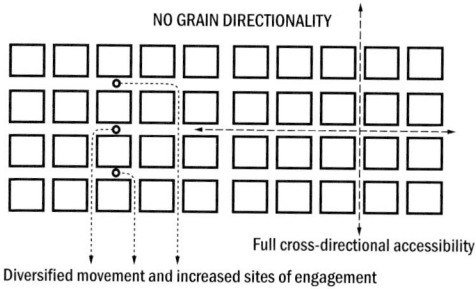

NO GRAIN DIRECTIONALITY

Full cross-directional accessibility

Diversified movement and increased sites of engagement

Urban block pattern: small blocks, equal sides

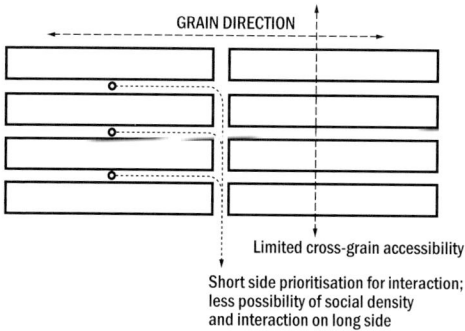

GRAIN DIRECTION

Limited cross-grain accessibility

Short side prioritisation for interaction;
less possibility of social density
and interaction on long side

Urban block pattern: long blocks, unequal sides

Grain and DIRECTIONALITY

through relating the configuration of buildings to open spaces (see *Figure-Ground*). Fine grain urban areas have many small lots and a diverse range of buildings with narrow frontages on small blocks. The streets and lanes servicing these blocks are closely spaced, narrow, and numerous. Visual complexity is high, as there are more exposed surfaces and individually identifiable buildings (see *Interest*) and the large number of small streets allow for greater freedom of movement and activation, variations in path and accessibility (see *Permeability* and *Choice*). In contrast, urban areas with a coarse grain contain larger-sized blocks with few lot subdivisions with streets further apart. Building frontages are usually longer, with less variation and few points of access. Movement infrastructure includes wider streets designed to handle large volumes of traffic. Due to the lower number of unique structures, visual complexity is lower, and movement choice is decreased.

Grain can also be formal or informal. Formal grain is part of a top-down development process and is often aligned with advanced planning and legal restrictions. The usual control mechanism is the alignment of lots, blocks, and movement infrastructure with simple ordering principles such as a strict grid or radial axes and nodes (see *Centre*, *Grid*, and *Node*). Informal grain occurs through a series of small decisions by individuals that then aggregate into a larger whole. They are characterised by irregular patterns of movement, large variation in block and lot sizes, and the absence of an overall spatial ordering pattern which increases interest but decreases legibility.

legibility

HIGH ←--→ LOW

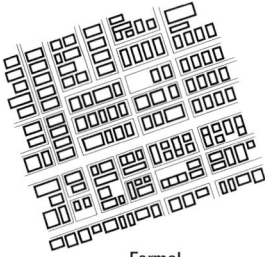

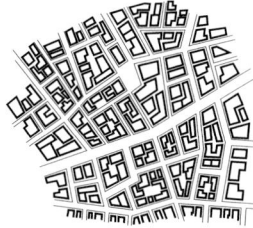

HIGH

Formal   Informal

FINE grain with HIGH GRANULARITY

complexity

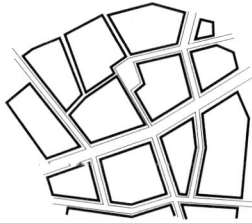

Formal   Informal   LOW

COARSE grain with LOW GRANULARITY

Grain CHARACTERISTICS

GRID

A GRID IS TWO SETS OF AXES ORGANISED into a larger pattern where each group is oriented in a different direction (see *Axis* and *MATBH: Directionality*). The two directions create a situation where each set will cross the other at either regular or irregular intervals. The result is the ordering of axes into a complex network of lines. Since grids involve points where axes cross, the concept also includes the idea of intersection; so, a grid can be thought of as a regular pattern of junctions or meeting points (see *Node*). Where lines are about movement, multiple intersections offer locations for activity and opportunity for engagement.

In urban design, the grid is an ordering principle used to organise urban form and structure urban development through street and lot patterns. The arrangement of street to lot arrangement is called the grid morphology. We use grids to measure, divide, and distribute land as well as to organise movement through circulation infrastructure such as roads and streets. The grid determines intersection locations, street lengths, and block sizes which relate to human movement patterns (see *Connectedness* and *Permeability*). In turn, this determines the granularity (see *Grain*) and the experience of moving through a city (see *Motion*). The major types of grids in urban development are regular, radial, and hierarchical.

Regular grids occur where the circulation infrastructure runs at ninety degrees to each other in a regular pattern. It is also called gridiron and does not meet in any central place or have a focal point. The streets and lanes in a regular grid form square or rectangular blocks creating a formal grain of either fine or coarse characteristics depending on scale. Regular grids often need to address topography and natural features, negotiating issues of slope and landscape features such as hills and streams, leading to deformation and distortion of the grid.

DOI: 10.4324/9781003254935-18

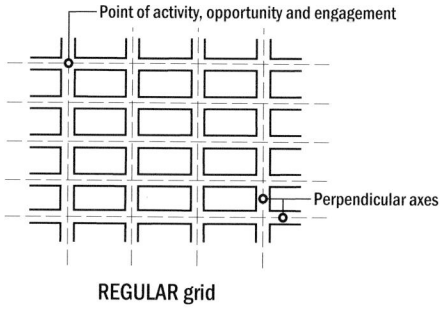

Point of activity, opportunity and engagement

Perpendicular axes

REGULAR grid

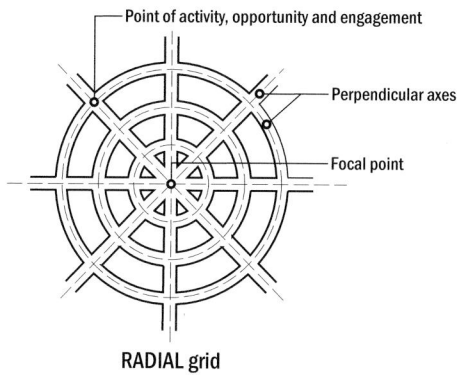

Point of activity, opportunity and engagement

Perpendicular axes

Focal point

RADIAL grid

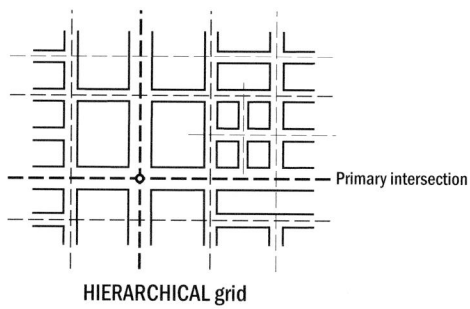

Primary intersection

HIERARCHICAL grid

Radial grids occur when the rays extending outwards from a centre are combined with concentric circles also moving outwards. The point where the rays and circles meet creates intersections and a grid structure. Radial grids bring simple hierarchy to an urban space, as the centre of the grid is usually occupied by an important building or public space (see *Centre*). Radial grids are often found in partial form in urban developments or as part of a nodal pattern overlaid on another grid structure.

Hierarchical grids can be based on either regular or radial grids and occur when axial lines are given different scales, capacity, and levels of importance. A hierarchical grid might combine different block sizes, have irregular spacing between axes, or overlay two or more grids in a more complex pattern. A good example of a hierarchical grid is a road system with freeways, arterials, collectors, local roads, and alleyways (see *Mobility*). Each road has a different speed of movement and a different volume and density capacity from the slow and low-density local road to the fast and high-density freeways. Hierarchical grids can allow for variability by supporting different grain patterns across the urban environment.

A grid is a structure of dispersal and a framework for urban expansion. It is through the grid that route options and choice is determined, making this an important factor for accessibility to a range of activities and infrastructure. Patterns of urban development expand through a combination of grid extension, distortion of rectilinear grid, as well as consolidation of the grid from larger to smaller block patterns and street hierarchy (see *Expansion*).

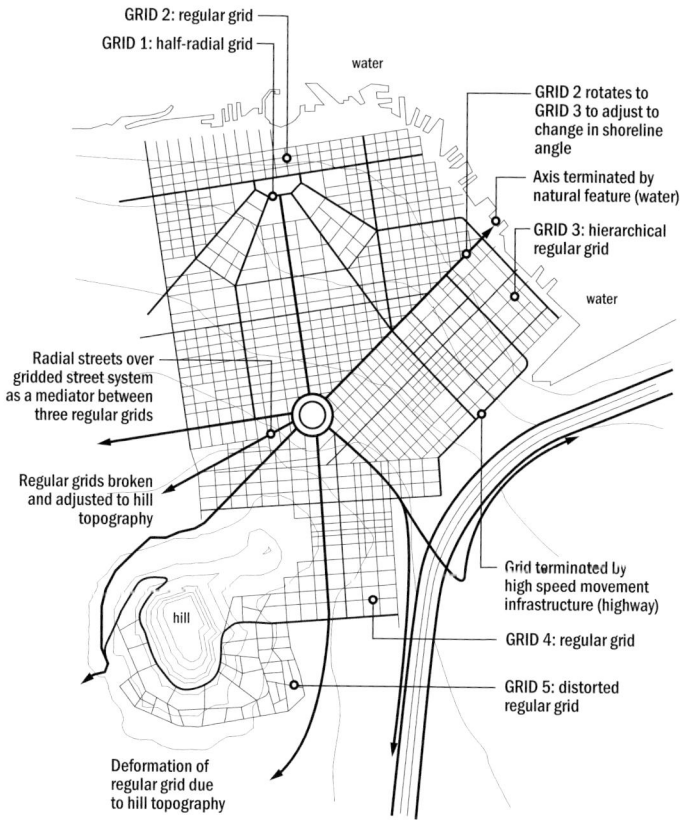

GRID 2: regular grid
GRID 1: half-radial grid

water

GRID 2 rotates to
GRID 3 to adjust to
change in shoreline
angle

Axis terminated by
natural feature (water)

GRID 3: hierarchical
regular grid

water

Radial streets over
gridded street system
as a mediator between
three regular grids

Regular grids broken
and adjusted to hill
topography

hill

Grid terminated by
high speed movement
infrastructure (highway)

GRID 4: regular grid

GRID 5: distorted
regular grid

Deformation of
regular grid due
to hill topography

Grid rotation and deformation in relation to natural features,
major circulation infrastructure, and urban hierarchy

Grid CONFIGURATION and DEFORMATION

MOTION

MOTION IS A PRIMARY SENSE for humans. We are aware of our body's position in space, its orientation, location of our limbs, and our self-motion. The ability to move is a physical act, but the idea is also used to understand other things. We use motion to describe abstract concepts such as time, lifespans, relationships, and other non-spatialised human experiences. Motion includes concepts of orientation, forwards and backwards, inwards and outwards, momentum, rotation, and relative speed. These are connected to how humans trace the movement of a body through space from a starting point to a destination (see *Path*).

In urban design, the quality and speed of motion affects our experiences and perception of the built environment. As we increase speed, we decrease our ability to discern details. A person walking has time to absorb more details of their surroundings. As a result, spaces with slow speeds, such as pedestrian precincts, walkable streets, and markets require fine grain elements, more permeability, and higher level of detail in material and construction (see *Grain* and *Permeability*). As speed increases, finer grain and details do not register, and the environment needs coarser grains and simpler details to be comprehensible.

Speed of motion is also related to flexibility and infrastructure. The slower we move, the easier it is to change direction and the less physical support we need to move. A pedestrian can walk on different surfaces, step sidewards, or turn around with ease. However, a vehicle has less flexibility and requires more infrastructure. The faster the vehicle travels, the more time, physical support, and a larger volume of space is given over to only motion.

DOI: 10.4324/9781003254935-19

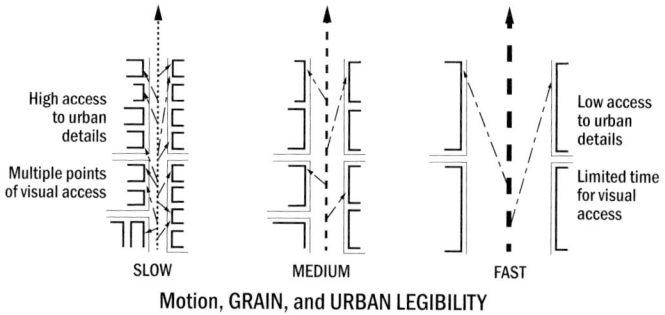

High access to urban details

Multiple points of visual access

Low access to urban details

Limited time for visual access

SLOW   MEDIUM   FAST

Motion, GRAIN, and URBAN LEGIBILITY

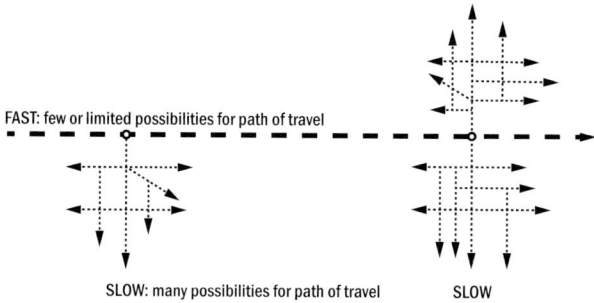

FAST: few or limited possibilities for path of travel

SLOW: many possibilities for path of travel   SLOW

Motion and PERMEABILITY

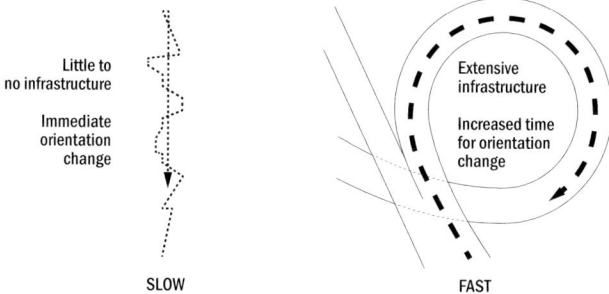

Little to no infrastructure

Immediate orientation change

Extensive infrastructure

Increased time for orientation change

SLOW   FAST

Motion, FLEXIBILITY, and INFRASTRUCTURE

NODE

A NODE IS A TYPE OF INTERSECTION which involves the meeting of two or more axes combined with the presence of attention that is provided by the concept of centre (see *Axis* and *Centre*). Nodes are locations where things converge and new elements emerge. They are places that draw us towards them because we believe something important is there. However, nodes are not isolated spaces or things but intersections which are part of a larger network of other nodes.

In urban design, a node is a centralised hub of density that concentrates activities and resources. Within a node, people are exposed to complex relationships between forms, open space, events, infrastructure, and movement, providing multiple perspectives (see *Compactness*, *Complexity*, and *Accessibility*). This provides options of movement and activities while supporting social density and opportunities through adjacency (see *Path* and *Choice*). Externally, a node is connected to other nodes through legible movement infrastructure which allows people to move easily between them. Successful nodes balance between legibility and uniqueness (see *Identity*), which allows them to engage but also influence the characteristics of adjacent urban areas.

The concept of node and nodal network operates at multiple scales within urban environments. Neighbourhood nodes might be several street corners and a local park, while district nodes could consist of a series of public spaces such as squares, community centres, and libraries. At the city scale, the Central Business District (CBD) and relationship to major commercial or entertainment areas would be a nodal network, while the regional scale would include multiple cities and towns as nodes along highways or railway lines.

DOI: 10.4324/9781003254935-20

1. Housing stoop
2. Local library
3. Shaded courtyard
4. Grocery store
5. Shared play area

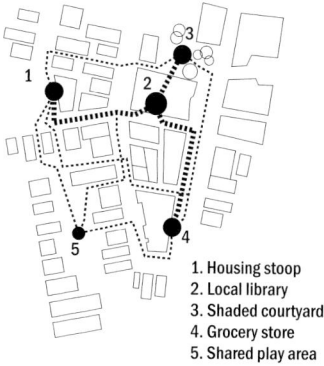

Nodes at NEIGHBOURHOOD level

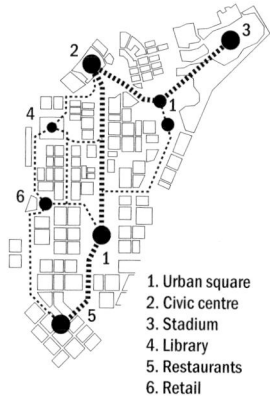

1. Urban square
2. Civic centre
3. Stadium
4. Library
5. Restaurants
6. Retail

Nodes at DISTRICT level

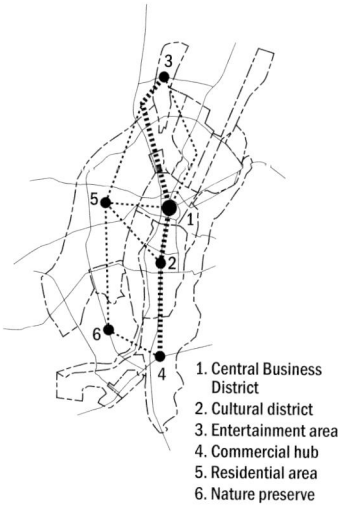

1. Central Business District
2. Cultural district
3. Entertainment area
4. Commercial hub
5. Residential area
6. Nature preserve

Nodes at TOWN/CITY level

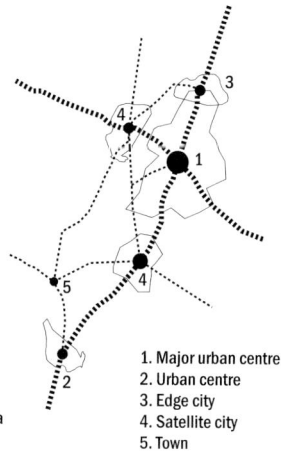

1. Major urban centre
2. Urban centre
3. Edge city
4. Satellite city
5. Town

Nodes at REGIONAL level
with CITIES and TOWNS

PATH

A PATH IS A LINE OF MOVEMENT as a projection of human intention. It facilitates the movement of human bodies in space (see *Motion*). The ability to move is a primary human sense, and we use the idea of path to understand how to get what we want, whether that is a location, desire, achievement, or experience. We understand movement as a point where our body starts, a line along which our body moves, and the destination that we wish to achieve. In this way, the concept of path always includes the ideas of source and destination, even if they are not explicitly expressed. A path is only a potential of movement until activated by the human need to connect a source or starting point with a destination or goal. Path is an important way we organise and experience the world around us for it to make sense. The primary tools for creating paths are axis and the related ordering principles of grid and node as expressions of movement (see *Axis, Grid*, and *Node*).

Urban design includes many types of paths at different scales and speeds. They are primary infrastructure used to organise urban massing through movement and connection. We might conceive of a public square or important building within an urban environment, an international airport on the edge of a city, or two urban centres within a region. While each of these urban objects or spaces are places we might wish to occupy as a destination, they are activated by considering where people might be coming from and how they might arrive by path (see *Activation*).

At a block scale, paths relate to the self-motion of the human body. As such, they are scaled to the experience of slower movement and limited by distance. Common paths at this scale are sidewalks, lanes, alleys, and walkways. As people are the primary activators for any human development, these paths are used to concentrate activities and create density

DOI: 10.4324/9781003254935-21

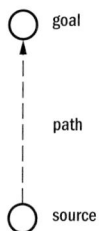

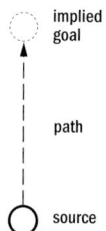

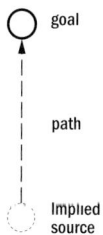

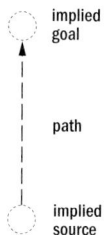

Path with SOURCE and GOAL

for destinations. Sources are residential units and parking concentrations, while destinations are resources such as libraries, markets, community centres, retail, entertainment, and workplaces.

At an urban scale, paths consist of mostly vehicular and mass transit infrastructure such as streets, transit line, greenways, and canals. These paths are the first foundational element that divides a territory or land into smaller units and organises them into urban structures like blocks (see *Pattern* and *Block*). Urban scale paths are fundamental to providing access to these blocks from various directions. They also are important for reinforcing specific land uses such as commercial, industrial, or residential activities through impacts on edge condition, figure-ground relationships, and activation. An urban path supporting industrial use has different characteristics to an urban path supporting residential use.

At a regional scale, paths operate at high speed and relate to highway systems, railroads, air travel, and other long-distance travel infrastructure. The role of paths at this scale is to connect urban centres with other centres and resources, including at a national and international level.

While we might focus on the path as an arrival experience, how we transition between paths of different scales and speeds is also an important consideration for urban designers as it is critical for human experiences. Choice of means of movement is also reduced as speed and infrastructure increases (see *Accessibility*). The shift from a high-speed, mechanised regional network to a local, pedestrian path network affects our understanding of urban details, path choice, and overall aesthetic experience.

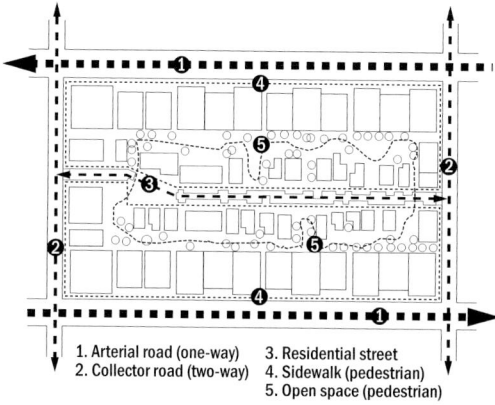

1. Arterial road (one-way)   3. Residential street
2. Collector road (two-way)   4. Sidewalk (pedestrian)
                              5. Open space (pedestrian)

LOCAL level

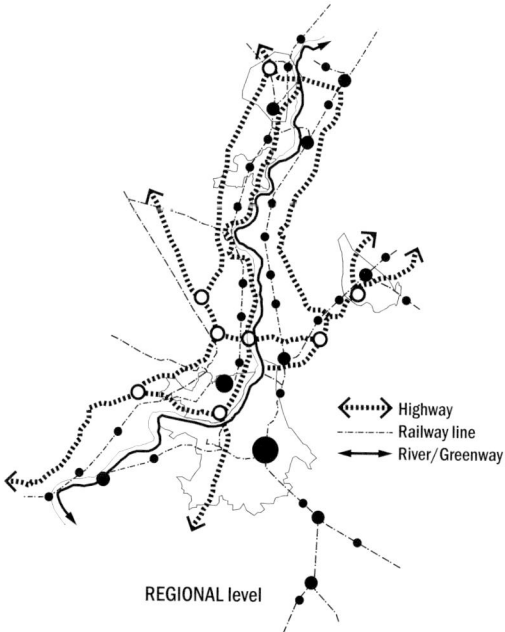

⟨······⟩ Highway
—·—·— Railway line
——→ River/Greenway

REGIONAL level

Path as SPATIAL EXPERIENCE and NETWORK

PATTERN

A PATTERN IS A TYPE OF REPETITION that brings regularity and organisation into our world and our experiences. We use patterns to increase our success of acting correctly in a situation and to decrease our stress of mental work when encountering a new or unknown situation. The introduction of regularity, which in this case means to be knowable through familiarity, allows us to make sense of the world. Patterns operate by grouping lots of little things into larger assemblies and identifying repeated sequences. The smallest part of a pattern is the repeated element called a *seed*. Once we recognise a seed and grasp how it makes a pattern, we use that knowledge to reduce the complexity of our environment. We can also extend a known pattern to complete partial areas or unknown content. More recognisable patterns are based on visual and physical information, but we also have patterns based on behaviour, activities, and events.

Urban patterns allow us to comprehend spatial distribution of elements and integration of activities through part-to-whole relationships. They include information about how much of something is present (frequency), where they are located (organisation), how close or far away each element is from one another (distribution), and what fixed relationships are present (configuration). Urban patterns are found at multiple scales focusing on different densities of human interactions. The smallest are usually found at the street-wall or block scale, while the largest are patterns of regional distribution of urban massing. We find patterns at the core of urban typology and morphology (see *Block*, *Typology*, and *Typo-Morphology*) and all ordering principles (see *Axis*, *Centre*, and *Node*). Formal patterns based on the physical relationship between building mass, open spaces, and movement infrastructure are expressed and recognised in the organisation and distribution of the grain (see *Grain* and *Grid*). This pattern is often described through two-dimensional information of building outlines,

DOI: 10.4324/9781003254935-22

Cycles of repetition (frequency + configuration)

pattern extension

1. Frequency (How many elements are present?)
2. Organization (Where are they located?)
3. Distribution (What is the distance between elements?)
4. Configuration (What are the fixed relationships?)

Pattern FORMATION and DEPLOYMENT

property lines, and circulation space (see *Figure-Ground*). Grain patterns are very large, but people experience them through the three-dimensional local information of *street height-to-width ratio* as well as visual interpretation of street-walls based on rhyme and rhythm (see *Edge*, *Rhyme*, and *Rhythm*). The pattern of building height to open space is important for human experience, as it affects access to environmental factors such as sun and wind as well as social factors such as view and visibility. Greater heights also increase a sense of enclosure, while lower heights increase a sense of openness (see *MATBH: Containment*).

While less visible, event patterns are just as important for the quality of an urban environment. Event patterns are ones that use activities, experiences, resources, and other more abstract but spatialised information. These patterns focus on how urban infrastructure supports human needs and how urban form makes human events easier to perform. Event patterns can range from dwelling entrance locations reflecting habitation preferences in a block, to the rituals of shopping in an open air retail in a market district, to the spatial experience of commuting every day across the region. Patterns offer comprehensible spaces for daily needs for access to resources such as food, leisure, education, and social engagement (see *Legibility*). Zoning is a type of land use pattern that organises land use into knowable configurations (see *Use*).

Patterns can create coherence through predictable relationships that reinforce each other, making urban life effective and efficient. They can also be used to design new areas or refine existing ones by applying previously successful patterns aligned with the same goals for the future.

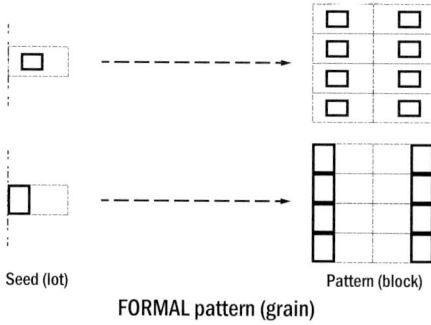

Seed (lot)   Pattern (block)

FORMAL pattern (grain)

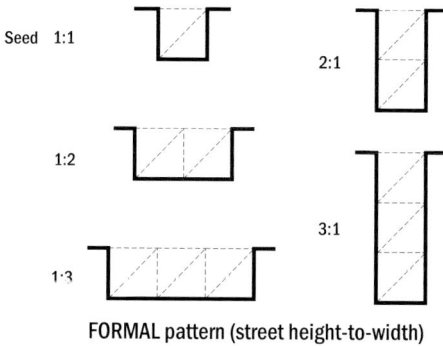

Seed 1:1   2:1

1:2

1:3   3:1

FORMAL pattern (street height-to-width)

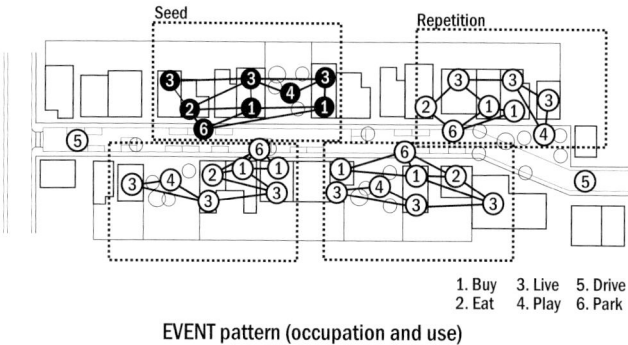

Seed   Repetition

1. Buy 3. Live 5. Drive
2. Eat 4. Play 6. Park

EVENT pattern (occupation and use)

SITUATED
NOTIONS

SITUATED NOTIONS
INTRODUCTION

70   DOI: 10.4324/9781003254935-23

URBAN DESIGN SATISFIES a human need for habitation. It supports this need through the design of relationships between various types of infrastructure, building massing and resources needed by people such as food, entertainment, work, and commerce. Urban design is useful when the physical built environment improves our lives as we live together in communities with increased diversity. We started with formal concepts as a foundation to understand how people engage mass, void, and motion. However, these concepts are also located in a *particular context* with *particular characteristics* leading to *particular forms* that respond directly to that context. This is known as spatialised and situated knowledge. The knowledge used by urban design involves ideas that engage movement, density, activities, and resources. Since these things and events occur in a particular location, their arrangement and distribution in space to create human urban environments is not arbitrary.

The first section introduced basic embodied concepts that we use to understand our environments through the way our bodies move, gather, and experience the world. This section builds on those ideas and extends basic concepts into situated knowledge of how we dwell in our communities. There is not a strict separation between these two sections, as formal concepts are also spatially located. However, situated notions use formal concepts by either extending their basic ideas, connecting two or more concepts, or grouping several concepts together. These ideas tend towards increased complexity and are more abstract. Their direct effect in the built environment is present as underlying factors but less identifiable.

BLOCK

A BLOCK IS AN OBJECT DEFINED BY flat edges and clear separation between itself and the surrounding environment. Interestingly, we think of blocks as solid objects rather than containers, which implies that the inside is inaccessible from the outside (see *Containment*). In urban design, a block holds the same conceptual idea of strongly defined edges and separation between inside and outside. Rather than a solid square object, an urban block is the smallest unit of land defined by mobility infrastructure, such as a street grid and expressions of privacy (see *Motion, Mobility*, and *Publicness*). Movement within the block is localised, while movement on the edges defines its boundaries. The most common expression of a block is a collection of buildings and properties defined by streets that form the edges. These edge streets connect to other parts of the city, while internal paths connect areas only within the block.

While we might consider a block only through a physical description, it also carries conceptual characteristics as an urban idea. A block is the smallest unit that expresses the fundamental human experiential qualities of the urban environment. It is within the block that we find the interaction between multiple urban concepts such as boundary, edge, centre, perimeter, frontage, use, privacy, rhythm, motion, and character in a legible and coherent way. A block is a manifestation of urban life framed by public street edges containing private local experiences.

Since a block is defined by strong movement patterns on its edges, it is always clearly bounded. The edge is also important for several other reasons. Due to the movement type that defines it, the edge is the most exposed and public part of a block (see *Publicness*). This affects buildings and building use in the block in different ways. We find strong fronts aligned with the edge to reinforce it (see *Frontage*). Often this is done through massing and reinforcing street-walls. The edge, and the events that occur

DOI: 10.4324/9781003254935-24

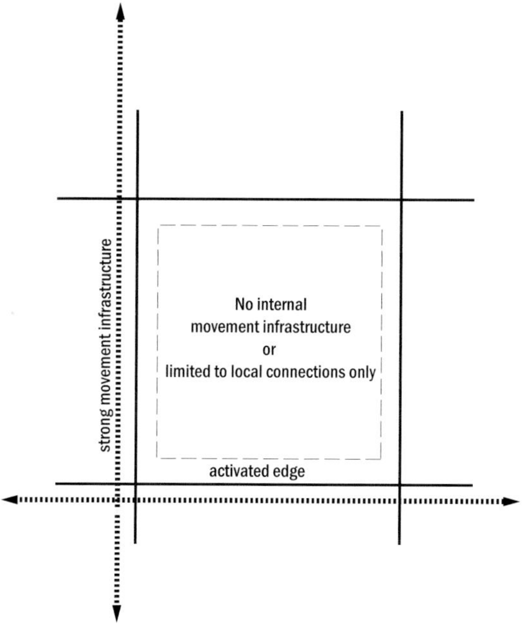
strong movement infrastructure
No internal
movement infrastructure
or
limited to local connections only
activated edge

Block structure based on EDGE and MOVEMENT

there, are also the most public, so we find entrances and physical access located there. Public events are found there in the form of lobbies, living rooms, retail, and entertainment activities. Private aspects of the block are pulled inwards to the centre of the block, where visual as well as physical access is restricted.

There are several different kinds of blocks, but they follow the basic pattern of movement infrastructure and publicness patterns that define edges of engagement. When all buildings are organised along the edges of the block, we have a perimeter block. A perimeter block has a clear public front with a strong street-wall and a private interior core behind the buildings. The continuous street-wall creates an effective street enclosure and active frontage (see *Activation*). Suburban blocks, in contrast, are characterised by pulling buildings away from the edges to create a weak street-wall. This is done to provide maximum privacy for the residents from all possible edges. In this case, the edges are still defined by movement infrastructure but less so by massing. A superblock is a collection of blocks where the street hierarchy is clearly defined through high-capacity arterial roads on the edges and roads within the superblock meant for local use.

While the shape and size of a block varies based on the street configuration, orientation, topography, parcels or lot subdivisions, land use, and building types, the underlying pattern of public edge and private interior is always present.

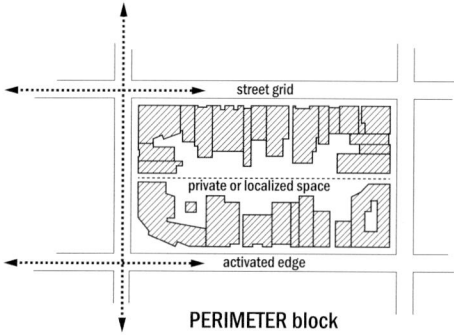

street grid

private or localized space

activated edge

PERIMETER block

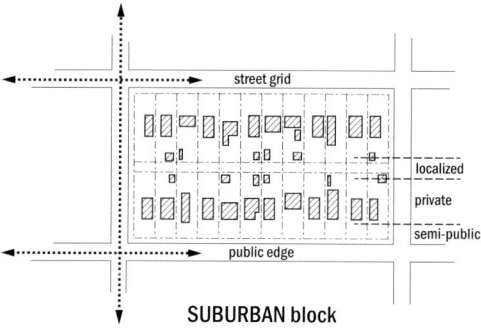

street grid

localized

private

semi-public

public edge

SUBURBAN block

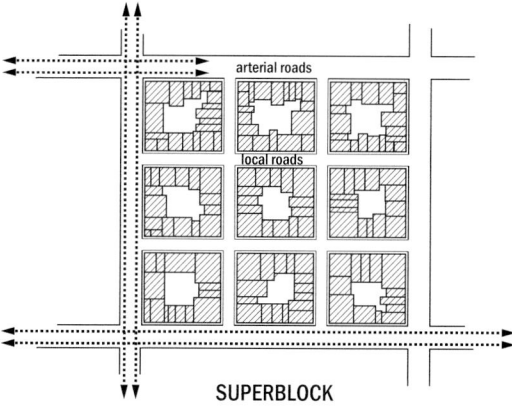

arterial roads

local roads

SUPERBLOCK

CAPACITY

CAPACITY IS THE LIMIT OF A THING. We understand the notion through the ideas of containment, volume, and fullness (see *Containment*). When a container is holding or carrying as much as it can and nothing else can be put in, then it has reached its capacity. If we try to put more things into the same container, it would not be possible. This makes capacity a threshold or a point that, once exceeded, triggers a different effect or event from before. The notion starts with the amount of things in a contained volume. In an abstract sense, capacity has a relationship to performance in which capacity is the maximum quantity or range of activity that can be achieved by an entity. The limit or the threshold becomes more important, as exceeding capacity can have negative consequences. We use capacity as an important notion of measuring, evaluating, and understanding sustainability.

In urban design, capacity is connected to *carrying capacity* of life in an area. It includes physical and spatial extents, density of people, physical development, land use, and activities. Capacity of a city determines its growth boundary as well as an infrastructure network to support the desired volume of activities and allowable density. The carrying capacity of a city is the maximum population that can be supported safely without damaging natural or manufactured infrastructure. Once the threshold of the capacity is exceeded, the natural and urban environment is irreversibly impaired, making this concept critical for sustainable development (see *Resilience* and *Stability*).

Four major types of capacities are used in urban design. *Massing capacity* measures how many physical structures could be in an area and how big they can be before stress is introduced to the environment. It reflects available resources, feasibility in terms of terrain and topography, technology, and economic values like land price and location. Crossing the

DOI: 10.4324/9781003254935-25

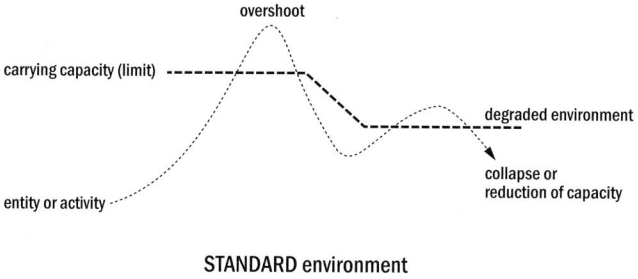

overshoot

carrying capacity (limit)

degraded environment

collapse or
reduction of capacity

entity or activity

STANDARD environment

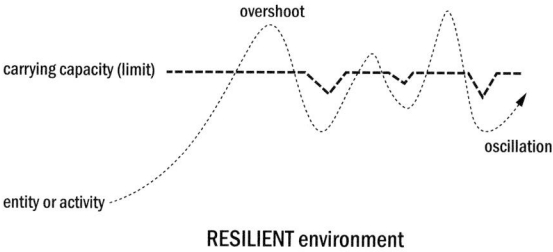

overshoot

carrying capacity (limit)

oscillation

entity or activity

RESILIENT environment

threshold of massing capacity can lead to overcrowding and congestion as well as irreversible damage to natural resources. *Zoning capacity* measures future development potential of an area based on physical characteristics, land use mixes, and event adjacencies. For example, zoning capacity projects possible configuration of the maximum number of dwelling units and non-residential uses that could exist in an urban area balanced with a specific amount of open space. This is based on the ability of that capacity limit to maintain a thriving environment based on the long-term availability of existing resources. When zoning capacity has been reached, it is not possible to add any more population to an area without conflict or social pressure. *Infrastructure capacity* measures the performance of infrastructure in an area. Specific examples could range from different types of transportation infrastructure like roads, highways, greenways, bike networks, and high-speed rail lines to drainage infrastructure dealing in stormwater and sewage. Performative capacity of transportation, sewage, drainage, water supply, and electricity are indicators of resilience and sustainability of an urban area. *Landscape capacity* measures what the natural ecological system in an urban area can support. It integrates human systems like a transportation network, property distribution, and built form massing with natural systems like geologic capacity, topographic capacity, and hydrologic capacity along with diversity of plants and animals.

Capacity provides an identity to an area by qualifying its performance and potential. It is a concept of understanding the necessary limits of human impact on the earth and a key factor in making sustainable and resilient communities. Enhancing capacity of cities to support existing and new populations safely under different future scenarios is critical to urban sustainability.

Decreased capacity
with increased slope
and landscape
features

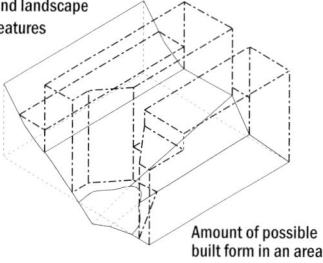

Amount of possible
built form in an area

MASSING capacity

Single family residential
(dwelling units per acre capacity = 3.4)

Multifamily residential
(dwelling units per acre capacity = 8.5)

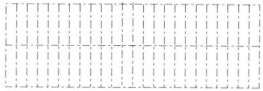

High-density mixed use
(dwelling units per acre capacity = 48)

ZONING capacity

Percentage of human volume per hour of different movement infrastructure
1. Pedestrians (21%)   3. Personal vehicles (2%)
2. Cyclists (10%)   4. Mass transit (67%)

INFRASTRUCTURE capacity

Water retention capacity: ability of a landscape
to absorb increase without deterioration

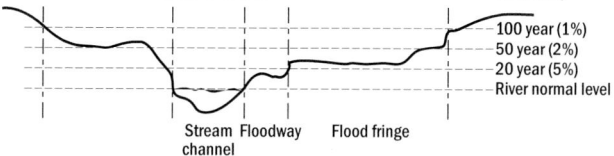

Exceedance
probability

100 year (1%)
50 year (2%)
20 year (5%)
River normal level

Stream   Floodway   Flood fringe
channel

LANDSCAPE capacity

CO-AWARENESS

CO-AWARENESS IS THE SENSE of being with others in a space. To be co-aware requires both the presence of someone other than ourselves (see *Co-Presence*) and the recognition of each other's presence. Co-awareness extends co-presence from passive occupation of a space to active awareness of others. This mutual and simultaneous acknowledgement is what forms the basis of social identities and influences behaviours and norms—essentially, it makes us who we are. Co-awareness extends the idea of simply being present into the ability to have direct contact and interaction with others. It is the basis of publicness (see *Publicness*).

The concept of co-awareness is based primarily on visibility through sightlines and exposure (see *Visibility* and *MATBH: Exposure*). Sight is powerful because when we can see something, we create a relationship between seeing and being seen. Co-awareness requires a type of visibility in which the sightlines are bi-directional, with both parties recognising the other. While sight is a dominant sense, co-awareness can be created through any sense as a possible source for the recognition of others, such as sound and vibrations, or odours. Often these sensory events support visual awareness but, if strong enough, they can stand on their own.

Visual co-awareness relies on convexity of spaces. A convex space is characterised by all points in the space being visible from one another (see *MATBH: Convexity*). As an urban idea, convexity has social implications that support publicness as those points in space are the possible location of people. An urban space, such as a square, street, or plaza, is made more public through increasing the possible areas of co-awareness which supports locations where people can be aware, see and interact with others.

DOI: 10.4324/9781003254935-26

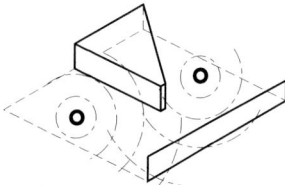

Horizontal reflected source

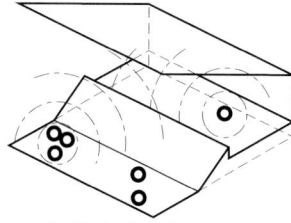

Vertical reflected source

Co-awareness through SOUND

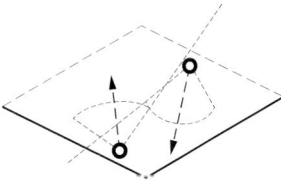

Co-peripheral vision

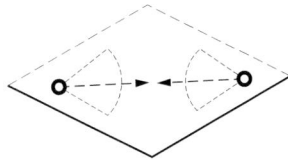

Bi-directional gaze

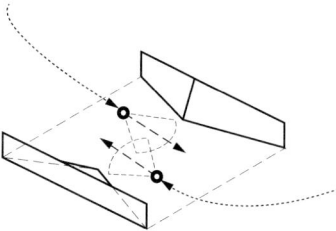

Paths influencing co-visibility

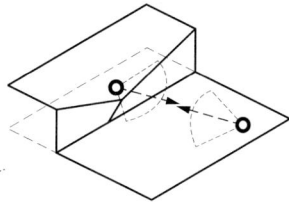

Vertical elevation and co-visibility

Co-awareness through VISIBILITY and PROXIMITY

CONNECTEDNESS

CONNECTEDNESS IS A MEASURE OF the relationship between spaces based on the opportunities created through accessibility. Accessibility is a spatial idea about easiness of movement and visibility (see *Path*, *Mobility*, and *Visibility*). Connectedness is also known as *spatial integration*, as it is about how voids are united to create a larger system. An area that is highly connected and well-integrated is one that provides a high level of inter-action between itself and many other areas. It allows for greater possibilities of engagement because there are more variations in paths and more destinations (see *Choice*). We can determine the connectedness of a space by considering how many other spaces can be accessed from that location and how easy or difficult it is to access those spaces. While connected-ness can be simply a measure of physical characteristics of a location, it is also an idea of social and economic health. Well-integrated spaces allow easy access to other people, resources, and associated opportunities, while isolated spaces make it difficult to interact with others. High connected-ness, thus, allows for diverse opportunities through interaction that lead to more transfer of experiences, goods, and resources, supporting social access and possibilities of public experiences (see *Publicness*).

In urban design, connectedness is primarily about path and visibility. These are activated through the organisation of the physical environment using ordering principles that are focused on movement (see *Axis, Grid, and Node*). Simultaneously, connectedness is reinforced or diminished based on what we can see and how much we can see from a location (see *Co-Awareness* and *Co-Presence*). When an area is connected with its surroundings, it allows for not only accessibility but also understanding of where we are and where we are going (see *Legibility* and *Place*).

Connectedness operates differently at various scales of urban devel-opment. At a neighbourhood level, connectedness is measured by the

DOI: 10.4324/9781003254935-27

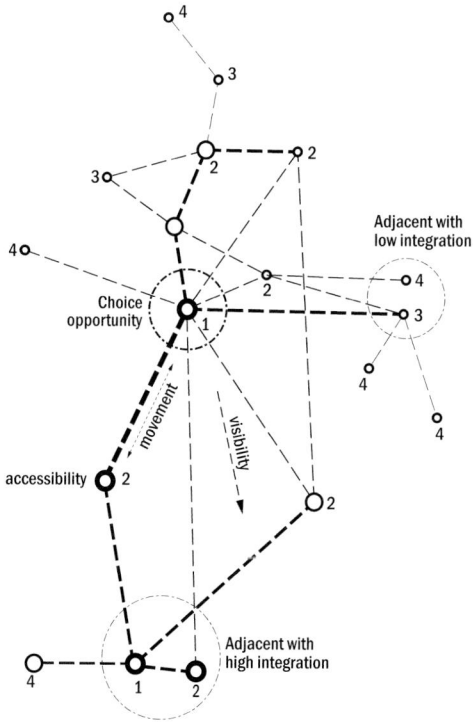

4

3

2 2

3

2

Adjacent with
low integration

4

2 4

Choice
opportunity

4

3

1

4

movement

visibility

accessibility 2

2

4

Adjacent with
high integration

1 2

1. High connectedness
2. Moderate connectedness
3. Minor connectedness
4. Low connectedness

Connectedness and SPATIAL INTEGRATION

number of intersections and how those intersections engage each other through visibility and path. For example, a well-connected neighbourhood node is situated at the intersection of multiple streets with visual access to and from many other intersections. High connectedness will make it a centre of attraction with retail, entertainment, and civic spaces like a market, park, or a plaza. Connectedness at a district level relates to the amount of permeability or the easiness with which we can move through different parts of an area (see *Permeability*). This might be expressed in the grid configuration with different amounts of broken and unbroken paths for thorough movement and visibility (see *Grid*). Connectedness at a city level reflects the amount of choice and accessibility between districts, with some operating as sources and others as destinations. A well-connected residential area, as a source, provides easy access to jobs, shops, and services in other parts of the city through varied modes of transportation. Finally, connectedness at a regional level is based on the directness, volume, and speed of the interconnection among urban nodes. A well-integrated region has multiple modes of access between urban areas that allow choice of movement by individuals. High connectedness at this scale will include multi-nodal networks connected through highways, mass transit, and green networks allowing cohesiveness and equitable accessibility (see *Balance* and *Coherence*).

When people have easy access to other people, it allows for more possibilities for engagement and exchange. Since highly connected spaces also introduce a range of choice of path and interaction, they are resilient, adaptable to change, and supportive of diversity (see *Resilience* and *Diversity*).

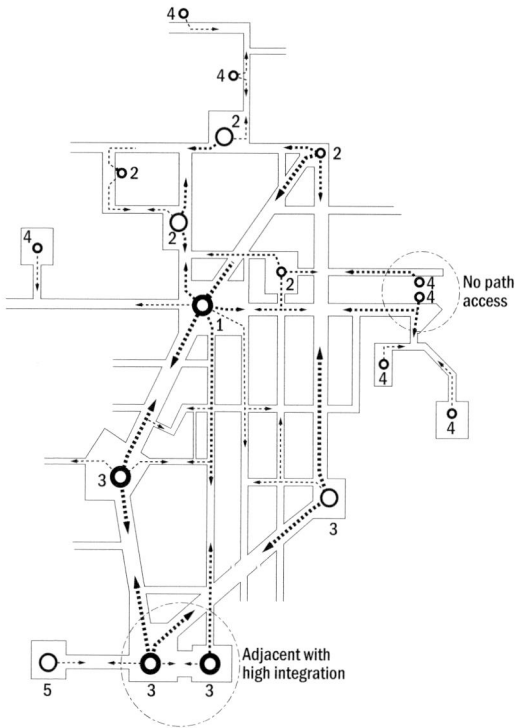

4

4

2

2 2

2

2

4
No path
4 access

4

4

1

4

3

3

3 3

3 3

5

Adjacent with
high integration

1. Many path choices
2. Several path choices, low axial visibility
3. Several path choices, high axial visibility
4. Limited options of path, low axial visibility
5. Limited options of path, high axial visibility

Connectedness, PATH, and CHOICE

CO-PRESENCE

CO-PRESENCE IS THE POSSIBILITY of sharing space with others. It is a social idea that involves the passive recognition of people and objects in a location. Where presence is the outward projection of ourselves into an environment (see *MATBH: Presence*), and self-presence is the inward experience of being in an environment, co-presence is simply mutual existence with others within a space. Co-presence does not require any direct engagement, interaction, or social recognition; it also does not imply a particular type of relationship between bodies existing in the same physical or virtual environment. It simply means that the possibility is there and that bodies co-exist.

While it does not imply interaction, co-presence does allow us to gain information and knowledge about others. This information might come from visibility but is just as likely to be from sound, vibrations, air movement, or smell. Each of these is affected by the composition and configuration of spaces. Our environments create the possibilities of interaction without dedicating how that interaction will happen.

Co-presence is supported by designed spaces that allow for tacit social engagement rather than direct action. It is a necessary component to extend into co-awareness, although this does not always happen (see *Co-Awareness*). In urban design, the idea of co-presence is tied directly to notions of publicness and privacy (see *Publicness*). It provides a basis for how we might shape environments to allow the sensing of others in the same space without requiring direct action and interaction. In a public space, this might be providing moments of withdrawal, rest, or oversight. These are moments that support being able to choose when and how to engage in wider social activity (see *Choice*).

DOI: 10.4324/9781003254935-28

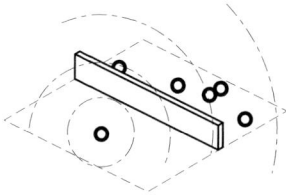

Single source to mass

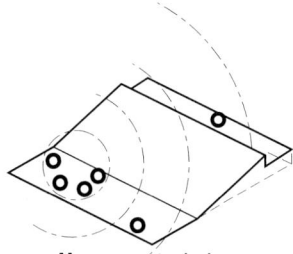

Mass source to single

Co-presence through SOUND

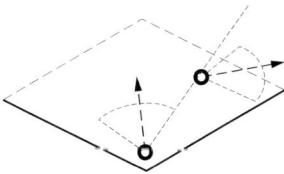

Peripheral vision

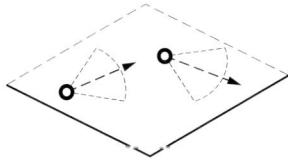

One-directional gaze

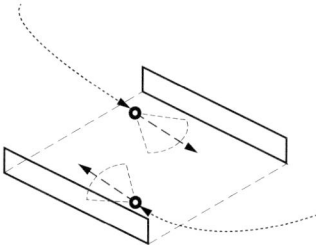

Paths influencing visibility

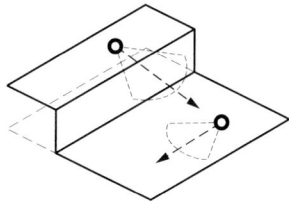

Vertical elevation and visibility

Co-presence through VISIBILITY

CORRIDOR

A CORRIDOR IS A LONG PATH that connects two or more things along a channel of linear movement. It is defined by strong parallel edges which are either real or implied. A corridor involves the concepts of movement, containment, and path with social interaction, integrating a strong axial experience with points of engagement and stopping. The linear channel expresses strong hierarchy, directionality, and identity, making the path equal to or stronger than the source or destination or other intersecting paths (see *Path* and *Identity*). For example, we often find corridors present as straight connections between nodes (see *Node*). The nodes act as starting or ending points, but the corridor will be equally important or even more dominant.

Urban corridors occur at multiple scales with different speeds of movement. At neighbourhood and district scales, a corridor is formed by two edges made of blocks. The side of the block facing the corridor is a front (see *Block* and *Frontage*). When a corridor has a high-density massing on the edge, it produces an urban canyon. Urban corridors, when present in grids, create hierarchy through strong directionality and increased importance. Speed of movement changes the nature of the corridor and its experience. A high-speed corridor operates as infrastructure that stresses mobility and connectedness. For example, a bypass road or highway creates a corridor around, across, or through an urban area. A low-speed corridor operates as a destination and an attractive experience. A High Street or Main Street acts in this way as a strong linear container with linked activities along its length. Corridors are also important green infrastructures, integrating systems of drainage (stormwater collection, distribution, and filtration) and sewage (movement of human waste).

DOI: 10.4324/9781003254935-29

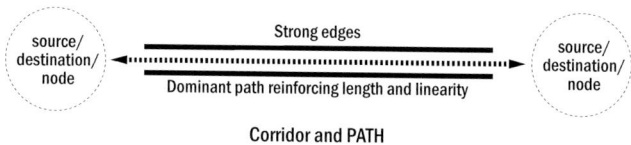

Corridor and PATH

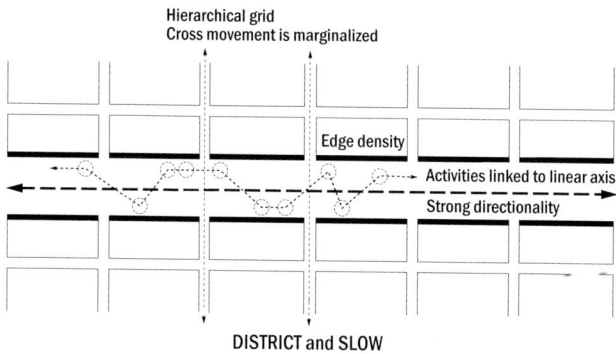

DISTRICT and SLOW

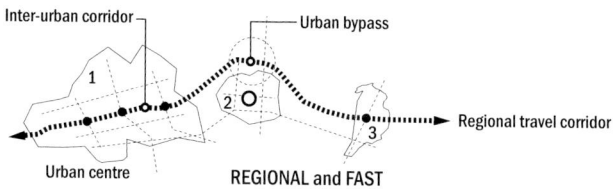

REGIONAL and FAST

Corridor, SCALE, and SPEED

DISTRICT

A DISTRICT IS an identifiable container with either a clear boundary or a strong core. It is an area of considerable size and extent (see *Boundary*), with a comprehensible sense of inside and outside. Paths and circulation infrastructure are important for the definition of districts as are the nature of its edges and the quality of the nodes (see *Centre*, *Edge*, and *Node*). Urban districts are critical elements of organisation and navigation of cities as they structure urban environments into manageable and distinct chunks. The internal logic of a district that starts with paths, nodes, and edges is reinforced by grain and material qualities which might include landmarks, historic elements, and traditional use patterns (see *Grain* and *Use*). Districts produce a clear identity which provides them with legibility and coherence through common characteristics (see *Coherence* and *Identity*). Since a district produces difference at a large scale, it makes a separate, distinct bounded space from adjacent locations. At a policy level, they form clear areas for specific types of development through certain incentives and regulations. As an experiential element for individuals within an urban environment, a district can be used as a reference for navigation and orientation.

The three primary organisational patterns for districts are line districts, nodal districts, and edge districts. Line districts are organised through a dominant axial line on which density and activity is found (see *Axis* and *Corridor*). The axis is usually a commercial street with retail, activities, and social interactions which would include restaurants, public buildings, and events with higher density than the surrounding area. While the street will connect to other parts of the city, it has a particular character which defines the district. The boundary of a line district tends to be weak, with unclear edges and gradual change in character the further away it is from the axis. Nodal districts are structured around one or more modes, which

DOI: 10.4324/9781003254935-30

Weak boundary
Strong axis

Major movement
infrastructure

Massing and activity developed on axis
LINE district

Weak boundary
Strong centre

Major movement
infrastructure

Massing and activity
developed at nodes

NODAL district

Strong boundary

Major movement
infrastructure

Weak centre

Massing and activity developed at edges
EDGE district

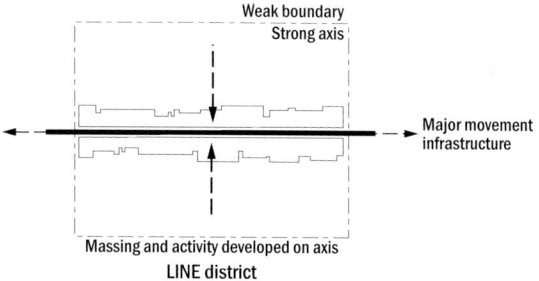

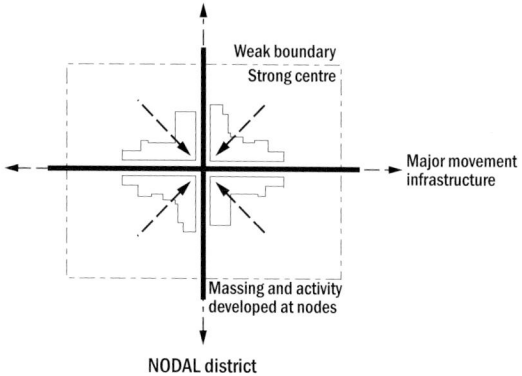

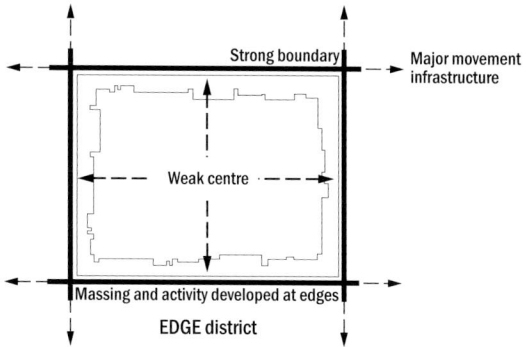

District TYPES

are usually a strong intersection or centre (see *Centre* and *Node*). Massing is clustered around the intersection or centre with high connectedness between the node and external destinations. Edge districts, in contrast, are defined by activity and massing on the outer edges of the area. The district is usually bounded by major infrastructure, such as an arterial road, or a natural feature, such as a river or coastal edge. Nodal and line districts are introverted with strong centres and weak boundaries. Edge districts are extroverted with a weak centre and strong boundaries.

Districts are used to define entities such as *neighbourhood* and *quarter*. These terms refer to districts with a particular focus, distinct underlying characteristic, use, or social composition. A neighbourhood is a type of district defined through social interactions rather than through land-scape features or commercial or political practices. In a neighbourhood, face-to-face social interaction is prioritised, and the district tends toward a dominant residential use. Neighbourhoods produce identity through belonging, concepts of home, community, and place (see *Place*). A quarter is a cultural designation that is socially constructed and usually connected to an identity of an ethnic or lifestyle group. As such, a quarter follows the historic and traditional pattern of cultural interaction as the basis for its formal composition.

Districts are important for identity and belonging and can be defined through events and functions (flower district, meatpacking district, financial district); cultural and historic memory (historic district); materials (Bricktown, cobblestone district); cultural experience (Bohemian quarter, ethnic neighbourhoods, or retail areas); natural geography (Waterfront, Lake District); and zoning (special incentive districts, mixed-use district).

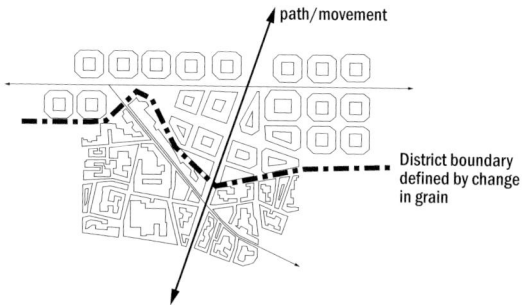

path/movement

District boundary
defined by change
in grain

District by GRAIN

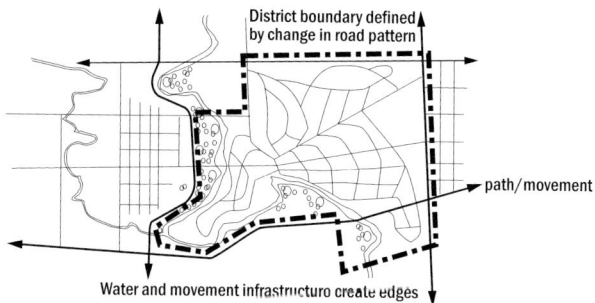

District boundary defined
by change in road pattern

path/movement

Water and movement infrastructure create edges

District by INFRASTRUCTURE

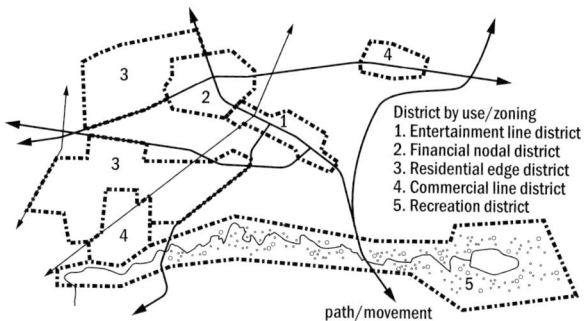

District by use/zoning
1. Entertainment line district
2. Financial nodal district
3. Residential edge district
4. Commercial line district
5. Recreation district

path/movement

District by LAND USE

FRONTAGE

FRONTAGE OF A THING IS a plane of engagement and the place of interaction. We understand frontage as a concept that comes from the experience of our bodies. Our front is the direction of our engagement with the world and the primary direction of most of our senses. This experience means that when we look to engage with something else, we also look for its front (see *MATBH: Front*). Frontage is the expression of front and the amount of possibility for engagement. The presence of a thing expressed through its front controls its accessibility, approach, and engagement along a path of physical or visual access.

In urban environments, frontage is identified as an important edge aligned to a path and property. It is the interface between the public realm of shared urban space and private or semi-private domain of ownership. In this way, it is frontage that determines the possible relationship between inside and outside as well as between individual and community.

Frontages can be passive or active depending on the frequency of openings for physical access (doors) and visual access (windows) as well as the degree of visual interest created through detail and variation (see *Permeability, Accessibility*, and *Interest*). A passive front has few or no openings and little visual detail with reduced sites of engagement between inside and outside. An active front has frequent doors and windows, while facades express interest through vertical rhythm and surface with variation in material, surface, and form (see *Rhythm* and *Activation*). Frontage is a critical aspect of engagement between people and urban space and has a direct impact on the quality of human experience in an urban environment.

DOI: 10.4324/9781003254935-31

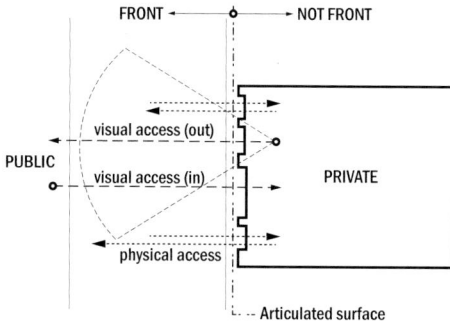

FRONT ← → NOT FRONT

visual access (out)

PUBLIC

visual access (in)

PRIVATE

physical access

Articulated surface

Frontage and ENGAGEMENT

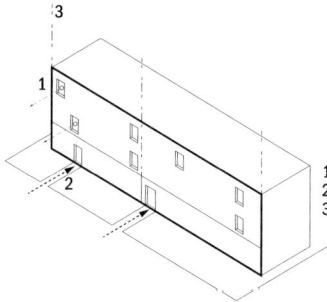

1. Low visual access
2. Few points of ingress and egress
3. Lack of visual interest

PASSIVE frontage

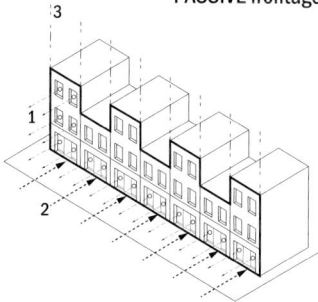

1. High visibility
2. Frequent points of ingress and egress
3. Visual interest through rhythm and detail

ACTIVATED frontage

LANDMARK

A LANDMARK IS a point of attention, orientation, and memory linked to movement and visual experience. It is a thing that provides us with an external point of reference as we move through a space. When part of the environment is different or considered important, we can use that distinctiveness to situate ourselves in both space and events (see *MATBH: Importance*). By doing so, we can understand where we are and how to get to where we wish to go. While elements that are recognisably different from their surroundings are important, it is also necessary to understand them as aspects of a larger network. While a landmark might be considered as an isolated element in an environment, it really operates as a node in a larger system of paths (see *Node* and *Path*).

In urban environments, landmarks can be either an object or a void, but they are always a figure (see *Figure-Ground*). They have a clear identifiable form in contrast to the surrounding area or background. This contrast is created through unique characteristics through its positioning; its physical attributes including size, material, colour, and appearance; and its historic and social memory creating interest and meaning for a region and population (see *Symbol*). Objects can be positioned in isolation with high visibility through open space or elevation, such as a fountain in a square, a radio tower, or a water tank. They might also be located at critical points in ordering patterns, such as at a centre or intersection of dominant axes. Landmarks can create attention through contrasting physical attributes or details, such as a complex brick building within an area of simple concrete or wooden buildings. They might also exist through past events or shared memories, such as a hundred-year-old bridge, a remnant of a mediaeval city wall, or an installation of religious significance. Voids can also create attention through difference and relief from the prevalent pattern. The major intersection of two important roads, an open public space next to a

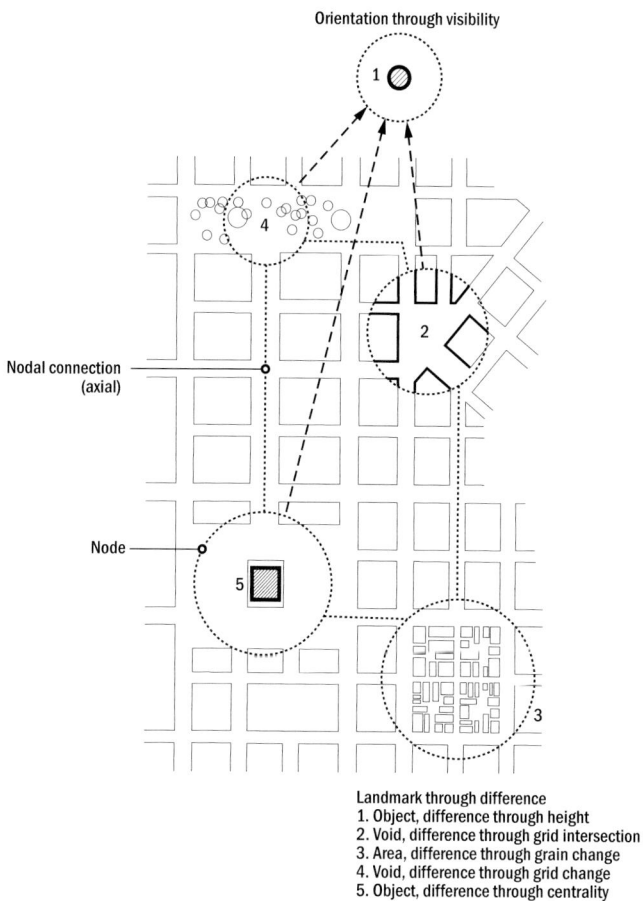

Orientation through visibility

Nodal connection
(axial)

Node

Landmark through difference
1. Object, difference through height
2. Void, difference through grid intersection
3. Area, difference through grain change
4. Void, difference through grid change
5. Object, difference through centrality

Landmark and NODE

historic building, and a park in an area of concrete or cobblestones all can create memorable spaces through difference.

While landmarks are created through individual objects and spaces, they help us in our orientation, navigation, and wayfinding. A singular landmark is connected to other landmarks through visual and conceptual paths, creating networks in our minds. The network allows us to navigate from one point of difference to another. This is especially important when navigating through unfamiliar areas. Landmarks, through their presence and visibility, help people see, remember, and select paths for their journey. The landmark is often a site of change in path or a place of choice with multiple options, with a clear change in quality or experience of the traveller, making it important for decision making in the urban environment (see *Choice*).

Landmarks can also express things that are hidden or foreshadow experiences not yet present. The presence of a tower of a religious building gives us hints of the open-space plaza adjacent to the building. A glimpse of brightly coloured canopies within that plaza suggests the activity we will find below them should we travel that way. They might also help us remember the weekly farmers' market or the annual town fair. Landmarks are expressions of interest and events situated in a specific setting. They also offer the possibility of future events and a promise of certain spatial experiences. Thus, landmarks play an important role in providing a coherent and legible experience of the urban environment (see *Legibility* and *Coherence*).

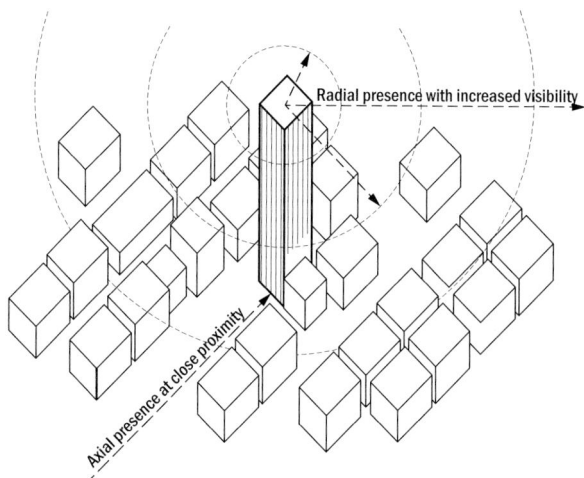

Radial presence with increased visibility

Axial presence at close proximity

Landmark and VISIBILITY

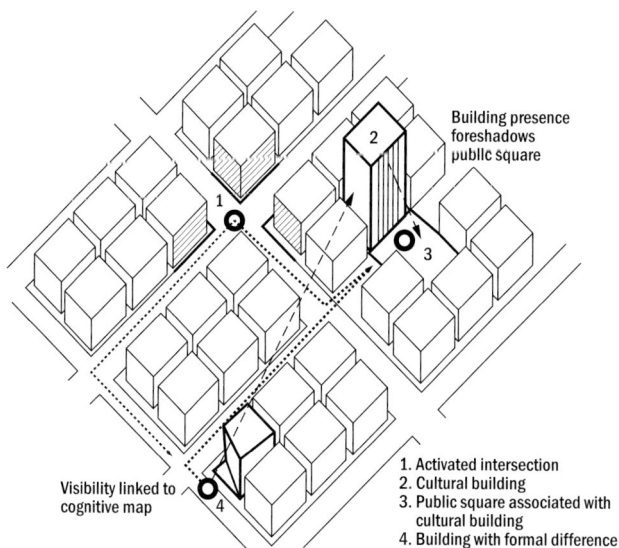

Building presence foreshadows public square

1

2

3

4

Visibility linked to cognitive map

1. Activated intersection
2. Cultural building
3. Public square associated with cultural building
4. Building with formal difference

Landmark, ATTENTION, and PATH

LEGIBILITY

LEGIBILITY IS THE POTENTIAL TO ORGANISE something into a recognisable pattern, which introduces understanding and meaning to a situation. When we scan a surface on which there are a series of marks, we associate those marks with known patterns of letters. The letters form words through a pattern of white space, and we associate those words with patterns of sounds (see *Pattern*). Those sounds are legible when their image, meaning, and context are in alignment. If we encounter a surface with marks but they are not related to any known letter forms, or they do not form word groups in coherent order, we cannot give them meaning. Likewise, if we are freezing on a glacier surrounded by snow, a sign that reads 'beware of fire' might be nonsensical. The same sign in a warehouse full of explosives produces a different degree of legibility.

In urban design, legibility depends on the composition and configuration of our built environment and their physical characteristics. An environment is legible when the perceived pattern of the spatial composition is interpreted in a way that has relevance to the way the space is to be used and the needs of the user. As we move through space, we read and gain information from the size, proportion, material, colour, rhyme, rhythm, layering, ordering, and relations in that environment (see *Balance*, *Complexity*, and *Coherence*). Our minds collect, organise, and store that information as patterns. When we later find ourselves in the same or a similar environment, the human brain is capable of recalling the stored pattern and applying it to the new situation. Legibility allows us to evaluate it and make decisions about navigating to a destination or finding a particular event in certain areas. When we expect that there *should be* a certain type of commercial venue just around a corner or *expect to find* a park or square marking the public centre of a town, and it is where we expect it, then that environment is legible. Legibility is the degree to which

DOI: 10.4324/9781003254935-33

Low legibility (text)

High legibility (text)

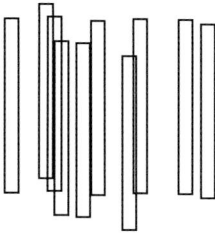

Low legibility (pattern)

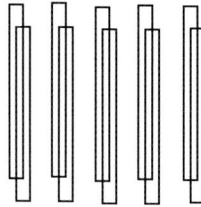

High legibility (pattern)

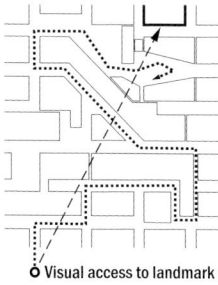

Visual access to landmark

Low legibility (path)

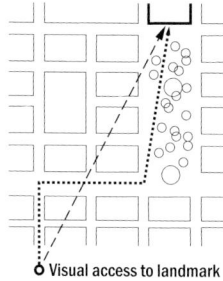

Visual access to landmark

High legibility (path)

the current situation can be organised into coherent and recognisable patterns in spite of complexity.

Legibility is an important principle for spatial navigation and wayfinding, allowing us to move through space safely and comfortably (see *Sensibility*). Wayfinding is the process of understanding orientation and location of our bodies, while projecting and following a route to a desired destination. It uses the relationship between spaces, things, and the underlying formal patterns to construct a mental image of our surroundings. When it is difficult to understand how a path connects one space to another, legibility is weaker. High legibility occurs when there are strong connections and clear choices between spaces (see *Path* and *Connectedness*). Within this process, comprehension of complex spatial layout and visual presence of urban landmarks are critical in orienting people and helping them make sense of their surroundings (see *Landmark* and *Presence*). Landmarks are central to legibility, as they mark decision points and offer choices between different paths with clear implications. Other moments of decision are intersections of paths and nodal points. When these are tied to clear ordering principles such as grid, centrality, radiosity, or node, our movement becomes more predictable through spatial legibility (see *Axis*, *Centre*, and *Node*). Urban experience is built on acquiring and assembling small bits of information gathered across space and time. This experience of interconnected experience and relational knowledge is not possible without legibility.

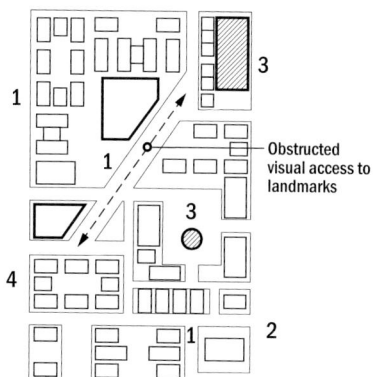

1. Discontinued street wall
2. Inconsistent path configuration (broken grid)
3. Limited presence of landmarks
4. No identifiable built form pattern

Obstructed visual access to landmarks

LOW legibility (urban)

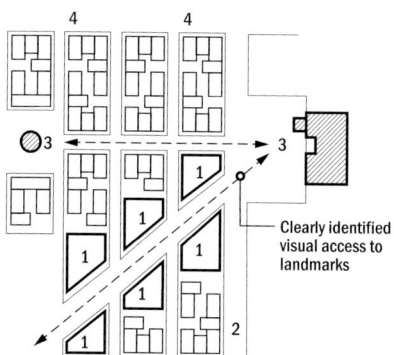

1. Continuous street wall
2. Consistent path configuration (grid)
3. Strong presence of landmarks
4. Clear identifiable built form pattern (block layout)

Clearly identified visual access to landmarks

HIGH legibility (urban)

MOBILITY

MOBILITY IS THE CAPACITY OF a thing for movement. It includes the ability to move as well as the sense of ease of that movement, the mode in which it occurs, and its speed. Mobility starts as a physical experience, but we use the same idea to understand abstractions such as social standing, employment, and occupations. In both senses, the act of motion is the core notion (see *Motion*). When we move, the factors of ease, mode, and speed are related to a goal. Since our sense of mobility is connected to a change in position, we find path critical to mobility (see *Path*). Path allows us to reach a destination and supports the desire to be somewhere else or in a different position.

In urban design, mobility is about the change of position of human bodies from one location to another. This is supported by infrastructure networks reinforcing interaction between urban areas (see *Connectedness*). Infrastructure includes the elements that allow people to move (path, roads, stations), and how they are arranged, including ordering principles and spatial patterns (see *Grid* and *Node*), the rigidity and frequency of those elements, their capacities, the supported speeds, and how much variation of path is allowable (see *Control* and *Choice*). Spaces with high mobility support easy and smooth movement of people with diverse travel options (see *Accessibility*). Paths of travel might include sidewalks and trails layered with biking lanes, personal vehicular traffic, dedicated taxi lanes, and ride-sharing networks, as well as various nodes for public transport, including bus routes, light rail transit, airport hubs, and multi-modal transit centres. Spaces with low mobility make movement difficult through a lack of connections, low legibility, and few choices in modes and speed of movement.

Movement hierarchy is an important aspect of mobility. This includes street hierarchy, the supported modes of movement within an infrastructural

DOI: 10.4324/9781003254935-34

LOCAL and SLOW | REGIONAL+ and FAST | LOCAL and SLOW

HIGH mobility and CHOICE OF PATH

point of mode change

LOCAL and SLOW | REGIONAL+ and FAST | LOCAL and SLOW

LOW mobility and LACK OF CHOICE

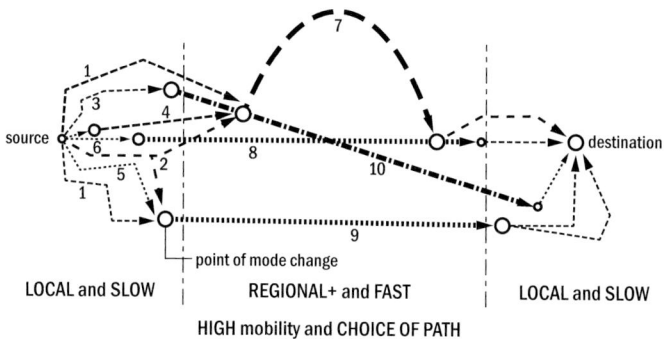

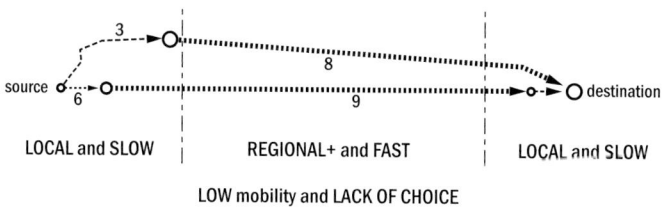

Mode 1: Public transit (lightrail)
Mode 2: Public transit (local bus)
Mode 3: Automobile (local roads)
Mode 4: Metro/subway
Mode 5: Bicycle

Mode 6: Pedestrian
Mode 7: Air travel
Mode 8: Automobile
Mode 9: Public transit
Mode 10: Regional/highspeed rail

MOBILITY CAPACITY and CHOICE

element, as well as the transfer between one movement system and another. Street hierarchy is the nested organisation of roads based on scale, supported volume, and speed. It ranges from slow, narrow, low-volume roads meant for local interaction, to very fast, wide, high-volume roads for long-distance travel. As we scale from local roads to regional connectors, the capacity and speed of the infrastructure increases, while diversity of motion options decreases due to the distance needed to be traversed within an acceptable time. We might find local infrastructure supporting a wide range of movement types, including pedestrians, bicycles, personal motor vehicles, and short-range mass transit such as buses. Regional movement infrastructure supports a narrower range of options with less flexibility, where we find personal automobiles and rail systems but less allowance for non-motorised movement.

As the movement infrastructure prioritises higher volume of one mode of movement, it becomes more restrictive to others. For example, high-volume pedestrian areas are difficult for motorised vehicles to navigate with efficiency and safety unless they are appropriately integrated through strategies such as separate lanes or grade separations. As vehicular roads get larger and faster, they become more restrictive to pedestrians and cyclists, decreasing choice and flexibility. Since different modes of movement have different types of speed, carrying capacity, and travel extents, it is important for mobility to ensure access to multiple modes as well as the smooth transfer between different movement hierarchies (see *Capacity, Permeability*, and *Diversity*). Urban areas with multi-modal transit hubs that integrate choices of long-distance, high-speed travel with local and regional access produce higher levels of mobility.

bicycle

pedestrian

NON-MOTORIZED

personal vehicle

light rail

bus

MOTORIZED

Mobility patterns (STREET/ DISTRICT level)

Regional

Metropolitan

Local

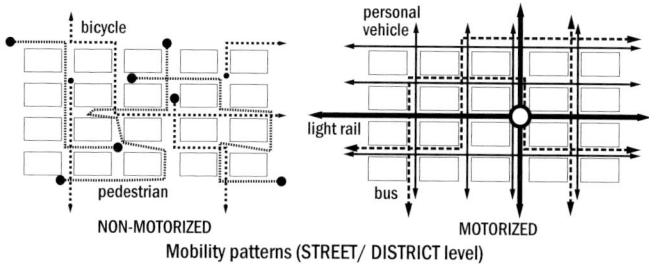

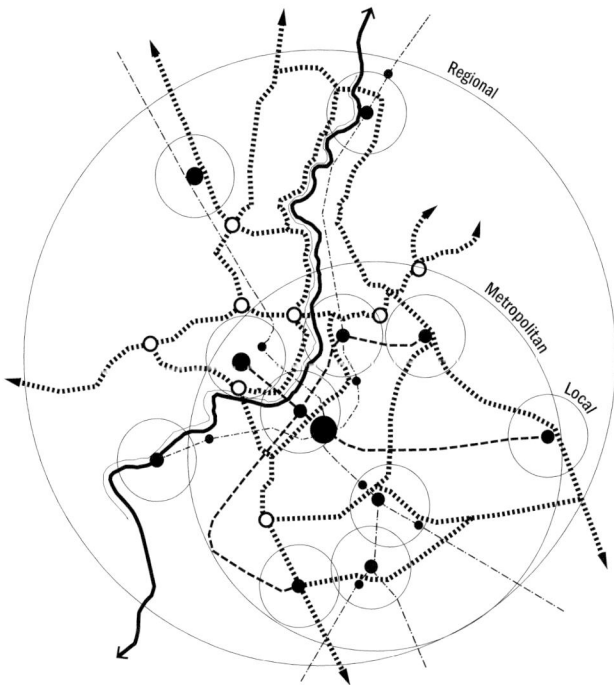

● Pedestrian movement (Range: 200 – 400 m)
○ Bicycle path (Range: 1.5 – 5 km)

◄▪▪▪► Vehicular road system(Range: 1 – 800 km)
─·─· Regional light rail/tram (Range: 10 – 15 km)
- - - - Intercity tube/subway rail (Range: 100 km)
←→ River/greenway

Mobility patterns (REGIONAL level)

Mobility SPEED, RANGE, and PATTERNS

PERMEABILITY

PERMEABILITY IS A MEASURE OF the capacity of an object or container to allow movement through it. It relies on the degree to which one open space provides access to another and how they connect to create a path of travel (see *Connectedness*). However, where connectedness can refer to the relationship *within* a container, permeability always refers to movement *through* a container. We might have a container with highly connected interior space that supports localised movement. However, it would have low permeability if there were no passage between edges allowing movement from inside to outside.

Permeability is also associated with *porosity* of a container or the relation between solids and voids within a bounded area (see *Figure-Ground* and *Grain*). This concept supports permeability when the available open spaces are connected as paths in a way that allows easy travel through the area (see *Path*). We can have a highly porous container (high open space to built form) with low permeability (open spaces are not connected to allow passage) depending on the size, shape, and degree of connectedness of the void spaces.

In urban environments, containers with varied degrees of permeability are found at multiple scales from a street-wall, block, neighbourhood, district, or city. A perimeter block with no public access between the street edges through the interior courtyard has no permeability, while a highly permeable district can be found with patterns of small blocks, forming a continuous and well-connected grid. Highly permeable spaces offer multiple and non-restrictive paths that increase the likelihood of human density, events, and activities through adjacency (see *Activation* and *Identity*).

DOI: 10.4324/9781003254935-35

Non-porous
Non-permeable

Porous
Non-permeable

Porous
Permeable

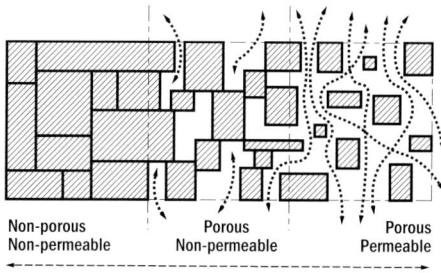

PERMEABILITY versus POROSITY

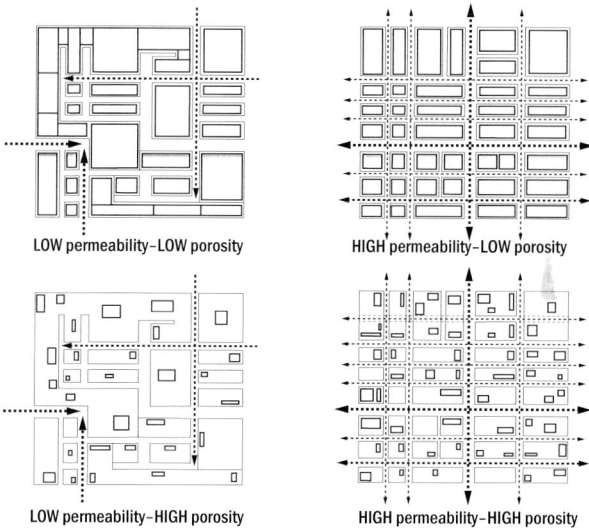

LOW permeability–LOW porosity

HIGH permeability–LOW porosity

LOW permeability–HIGH porosity

HIGH permeability–HIGH porosity

DISTRICT permeability

RHYME

RHYME IS A PATTERN THAT uses similarity to create a relationship between things in the world (see *Pattern*). When we hear or see a sequence of things that look similar but are not exactly the same, the close similarity creates a grouping that we associate with a rhyme pattern (see *MATBH: Similarity*). While we think of rhymes as being related to spoken or written language, the same notion is present in visual information and events.

In urban design, rhymes are based on shapes we see in our built environment. Since the type of information we use to recognise a rhyme is visual, the rhyme tends to be limited to visualisation of profiles of urban elements. When we recognise similarity in elements in a localised area, those elements are grouped into a simple pattern to produce legibility (see *Legibility*). Rhymes are commonly recognised in street-walls, urban edges, and corridors (see *Edge* and *Corridor*). These elements might be window or door shapes on a facade, entrance profiles or locations, building silhouettes, massing proportions, material treatment and details, block grain expressed through property width and frontage, or urban objects such as benches, lights, kiosks, or bollards.

Rhyme brings order and sense to our environment by creating a distinct location from a series of parts (see *Place*). Rhyme is important to create coherence in a location without strict repetition. As the exact composition of the rhyme will differ from one location to another, it allows us to identify uniqueness to that particular instance even while using a limited number of elements (see *Interest*). This creation of complexity through similarity leads to distinct identity in urban areas.

DOI: 10.4324/9781003254935-36

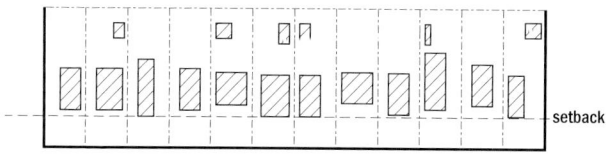

Similar but not identical building width and height
Similar gable roofs with varying slopes and edges

Rhyme and BUILDING SILHOUETTE patterns

Similar window and door shapes
Consistent base-middle-top hierarchy present but varying proportions

top

middle

base
similarity

Rhyme, BUILDING OPENINGS, and FACADE patterns

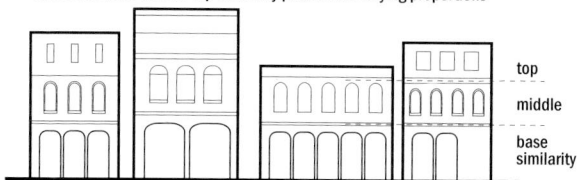

Identical lot size, setback and frontage
Similar but not identical building positioning, massing and footprint

setback

Rhyme and GRAIN patterns

Identical buildings
Different material surfaces and treatments

Rhyme and MATERIALITY patterns

RHYTHM

RHYTHM IS ACHIEVED BY grouping things into a sequence that recurs at a regular interval (see *Pattern*). A 'thing' can be an object, space, attribute, or event and the pattern created is periodic or repeated as part of a cycle. Rhythm helps us make sense of a situation by ordering solid objects (or tones) and open spaces (or silences) into moments of attention. Those moments reinforce other types of information present (see *Legibility* and *Coherence*).

Rhythm in urban design is found in the repeated and layered relationships between objects and space in the built environment. These *formal rhythms* are static, visual interpretations of urban compositions, often experienced in street-walls or exposed fronts accessible to public view (see *Edge* and *Frontage*). When we break down a large building facade on the street into regular intervals of bays, the repetitive pattern of a series of stepped entries into row-houses or the consistent space between trees on the sidewalk framing entrances or openings, we create a rhythm.

Formal rhythms support *event rhythms*, which are human activities that occur over and over again. Event rhythms range in type, extent, focus, and frequency. Some events can have a daily rhythm tied to basic human needs, such as everyday patterns of eating, social gathering, or traffic volume changes due to standardised working hours. Others can be sporadic, such as a weekly farmers' market that provides access to fresh food and reinforces the identity of a district. Still others are seasonal, with one or two events during the year, yet attracting large gatherings. These periodic events are reflected in urban spatial patterns which form our built environment.

DOI: 10.4324/9781003254935-37

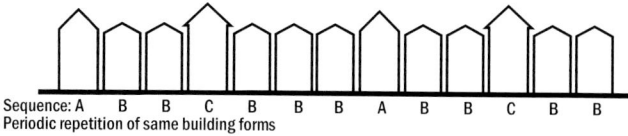

Sequence: A B B C B B B A B B C B B
Periodic repetition of same building forms

Rhythm and BUILDING SILHOUETTE patterns

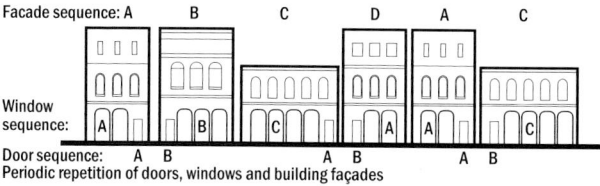

Facade sequence: A B C D A C

Window sequence: A B C A A C

Door sequence: A B A B A B
Periodic repetition of doors, windows and building façades

Rhythm, BUILDING OPENINGS, and FACADE patterns

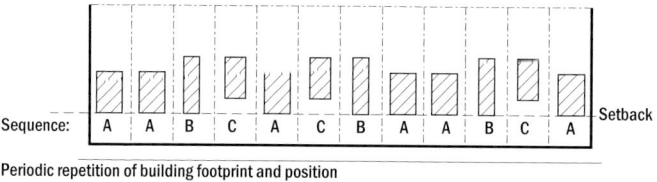

Sequence: A A B C A C B A A B C A Setback

Periodic repetition of building footprint and position

Rhythm and GRAIN patterns

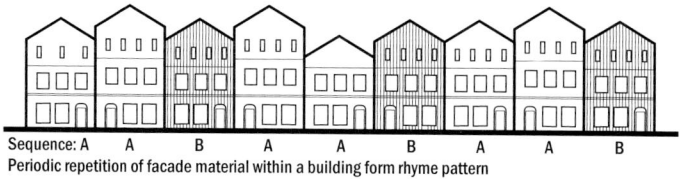

Sequence: A A B A A B A A B
Periodic repetition of facade material within a building form rhyme pattern

Rhythm and MATERIALITY patterns

SPACE

SPACE IS THE AREA AROUND EVERYTHING that exists. It is often considered to be abstract—a boundless and continuous three-dimensional expanse that makes up our reality. Inside this expanse, we find all the objects and substances with which people can interact. Since space does not have any content or apparent use that humans can perceive, we consider it to be empty. We think about space as something we can fill or an extent that is available to us to occupy and use. In this way, space is defined as an endless, unbounded, generic, and limitless universal resource. However, when engaged by people, space is only ever experienced as finite, bounded, and situated.

In urban design, space is finite and bounded because the only way we experience space is through the presence of an edge which defines a boundary and suggests an enclosure (see *Boundary* and *Edge*). A boundary allows one part of space to be made distinct from another. This allows it to be measured and described through dimension, given an orientation, and assigned different qualities (see *MATBH: Objectification*). These basic descriptions might include its surface regularity or relative scale, or its tendency towards flatness or volume as well as concavity or convexity (see *MATBH: Convexity*). As a bounded volume, space is understood as a series of containers rather than a continuum (see *Containment*). Things describing the separation of one part of space from another might be objects and buildings but are also equally likely to be human events and activities.

Bounded space is situated as each perceived container has a specific composition, scale, and arrangement of forms even without a distinct identity. The bounded and situational characteristics of a space, based only on the arrangement of physical elements, influence how that space might be used by people in a location. They affect how we enter and exit the contained space, the types of paths that are possible, how gathering

DOI: 10.4324/9781003254935-38

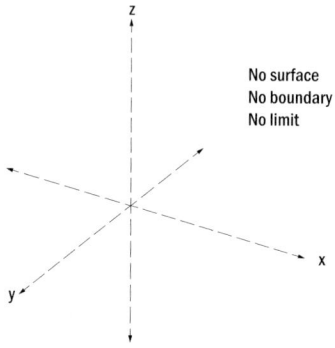

No surface
No boundary
No limit

UNBOUNDED and INFINITE space

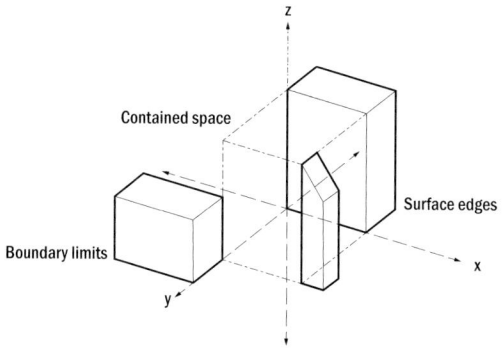

Contained space

Surface edges

Boundary limits

BOUNDED and FINITE space

Space and BOUNDARY

is supported, what activities might be able to take place, where and how people can have access to other people, and which areas are visible or exposed to other areas (see *Path*, *Co-Awareness*, *Visibility*, *Accessibility*, and *Publicness*). Each of these factors has a social effect through supporting the position, orientation, and accessibility of individual human bodies to one another. For example, the physical dimension, perceived edges, and physical characteristics of a specific neighbourhood street reflects whether the street is used as a private residential or public commercial street. This includes the definition of the edges but also how the space is ordered between inside and outside (see *Axis*, *Centre*, and *Node*), grain patterns and orientation patterns (see *Grain* and *Frontage*), sightlines, paths, and accessibility through doors, windows, and passages (see *Path*, *Permeability*, *Visibility*, and *Control*). The surfaces that define the nature of each spatial container limit the affordances present in that location, which are the possibilities an environment offers to the people who occupy it.

Space can be considered neutral only until it is bounded and situated. Once space is perceived through a particular arrangement, it is one of the most fundamental concepts that suggests the potential of shared human experiences through physical composition. It holds a significant amount of social information that is aligned with the position, orientation, and visibility of human bodies. At the same time, space does not inherently contain any content based on social agreements or complex human narratives such as cultural meaning, memories, geo-political identities, and value-based positions (see *Place*).

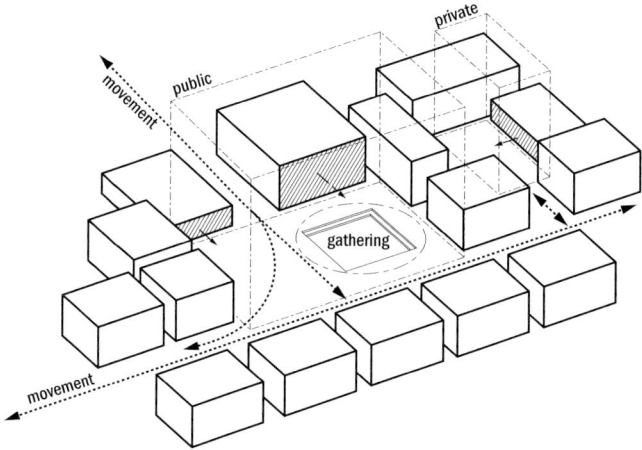

CONFIGURATION 1: Medium public square with private court

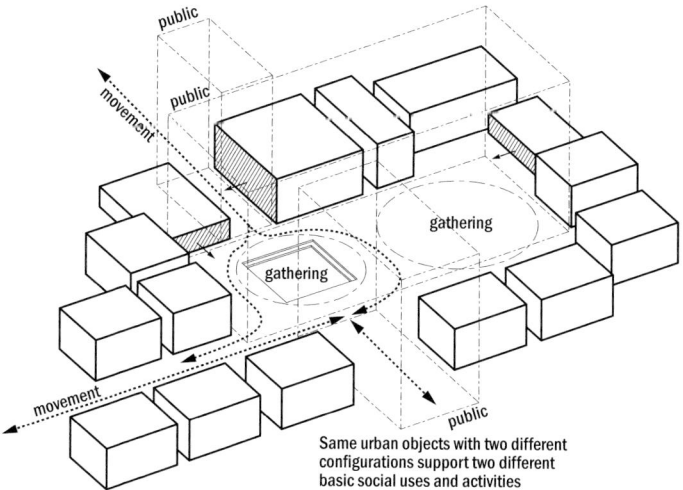

Same urban objects with two different configurations support two different basic social uses and activities

CONFIGURATION 2: Large public square with indirect circulation

Space, CONFIGURATION, and SOCIAL INFORMATION

VISIBILITY

VISIBILITY IS THE CAPACITY to see or be seen. This is a primary way for humans to understand and know the world around us. Humans extend the concept of seeing to other types of knowledge such as understanding ('I see what you mean'), making abstract concepts concrete ('I saw the idea taking shape'), and creating relationships ('their eyes locked in understanding'). We also consider seeing as a type of touching with all the effects of physical contact ('their gaze went through me'). Visibility characterises how exposed one thing is to another, whether it is an organism, object, event, or idea. As a physical experience, visibility is affected by aspects of our environment that support views such as scale, elevation, orientation, directionality, and the solid-void relationship (see *Axis*, *Figure-Ground*, and *Frontage*). It is also aligned with light and darkness, as light is critical for human sight.

The two types of visibility important to urban design are axial visibility and field visibility. Axial visibility is the uninterrupted view possible in one direction along a narrow, straight sightline. It includes either a focal point through linear relationships between urban elements or a strong, narrow edge condition (see *Corridor* and *Landmark*). Field visibility is the range of view possible through the field of human vision. In an urban environment, it is expansive with a view of the horizon, where we see multiple elements in a horizontal relationship but without a focal point. Both field and axial visibility are involved in creation of a vista or a significant view with an interest (see *Interest*). A vista in a field condition stresses a horizontal expanse and reinforces the horizon. When a vista is part of an axial condition, it is called a terminated vista and is created by placing a significant urban object at the end of a strong visual axis. In both cases, a vista produces a scene or prospect that becomes an extension of the space from which it is seen. The result is the increase in visual richness and quality of experience in the space from which it is viewed.

DOI: 10.4324/9781003254935-39

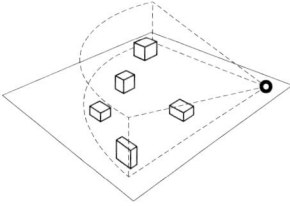

FIELD visibility

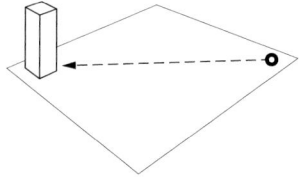

AXIAL visibility

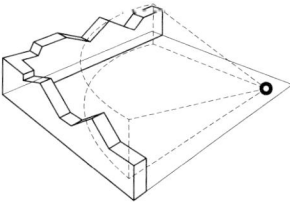

Spatial termination through field

VISTA

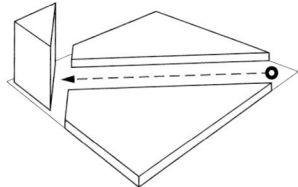

Spatial termination through axis

Terminated VISTA

In urban environments, visibility at multiple scales is not just about exposure. It also relates to construction of relationships, perceived comfort, and safety, as well as sensible and coherent environments (see *Legibility*). When we shape spaces and objects with direct sightlines to each other, we imply a relationship. Two urban squares with axial visibility will be naturally associated through visual connection, often reinforcing a path connection for movement. Similarly, two landmarks that can entirely or partially 'see' each other, even across some distance, project a relationship with promise of destination through presence of events, activity, and opportunities for public interaction. Sightlines allowing a glimpse of where we wish to go or providing access to patterns of organisation help people situate themselves (see *Path*). At a street and block scale, sightlines are important for safety at intersections, especially to address mobility of different speeds and capacities. When an area has multiple sightlines from various places, it also tends to increase the sense of perceived safety. Visibility also has an effect on whether a space is considered to be public or private through the association with presence and awareness of others (see *Co-Awareness, Co-Presence,* and *Publicness*). At a district or urban scale, we use visible aspects of the environment to allow us to understand destinations and produce a localised identity (see *Identity*).

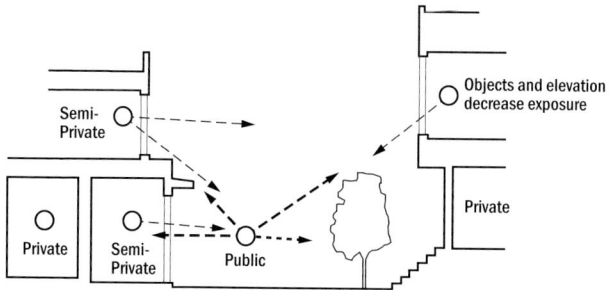

Multiple sightlines from inside to outside reinforcing
on-street publicness and indoor privacy

Visibility and PUBLICNESS

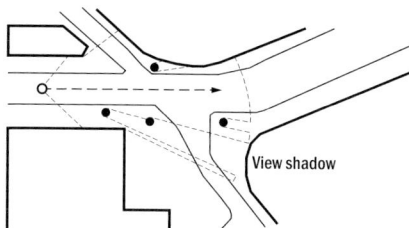

Visibility reduced by urban objects (buildings,
lights, signs, people) and view angles

Visibility and SAFETY

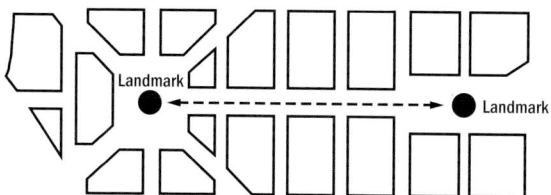

Visual connection between landmarks implied relationship and path

Visibility and RELATIONSHIP

WALKABILITY

WALKABILITY IS A MEASURE OF HOW an environment supports the human experience of pedestrian movement. It is focused on our experience of the world through our senses and ease of motion. The experience of moving through space, and how we judge that movement, is affected by our surroundings, what information is available to our senses, and what opportunities are easily accessible. A major factor in what we can see, hear, smell, and feel as we move from one location to another is the spatial positioning of events and their support through urban form and infrastructure. We use this primary knowledge to map a path to a destination (see *Sensibility*), highlight possible engagement with other people (see *Publicness*), and judge our sense of safety through adjacency and exposure (see *Co-Awareness* and *Visibility*).

Walkability is not just the ability to walk easily in a location. The concept includes how the compositional arrangement of the built environment and mix of functional uses support the positive experience of walking and encourage higher access to resources (see *Accessibility*, *Use*, and *Diversity*). This experience is complex, dynamic, and multi-dimensional. It involves different layers of the environment starting with density and arrangement of buildings (see *Grain*), diversity and mix of activities (see *Use*), presence and adjacency of destinations (see *Path* and *Connectedness*), and connectivity and proximity of movement infrastructure (see *Locality*). These layers then engage more complex factors such as the role of climate and topography, perception of safety and security through urban configuration, and the amount of opportunities available to inhabitants in relation to human density and variation of use (see *Compactness*, *Density*, *Co-Presence*, and *Activation*).

As a local experience, walkability relies on high dwelling density, mixed land use, and small block sizes (fine grain) connected by a continuous

DOI: 10.4324/9781003254935-40

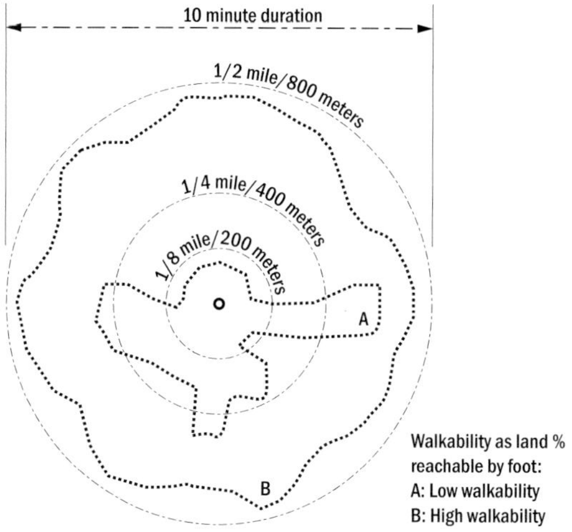

10 minute duration

1/2 mile/800 meters

1/4 mile/400 meters

1/8 mile/200 meters

A

B

Walkability as land %
reachable by foot:
A: Low walkability
B: High walkability

Walkability DISTANCE and REACHABILITY

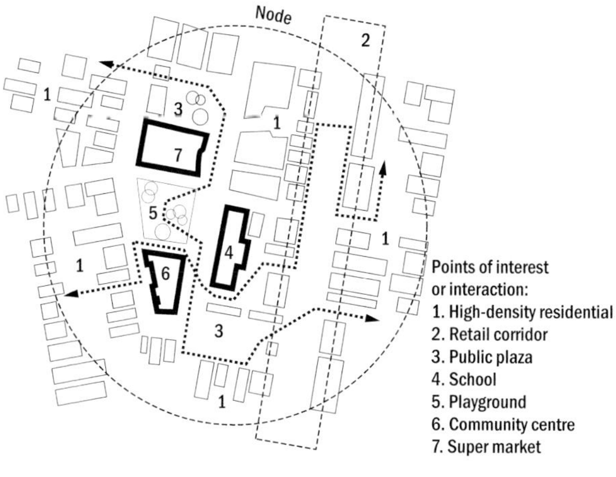

Node

2

1

3

7

1

5

4

6

1

3

1

1

Points of interest
or interaction:
1. High-density residential
2. Retail corridor
3. Public plaza
4. School
5. Playground
6. Community centre
7. Super market

Walkability distances by PATH and DESTINATION

pedestrian network with high choice (see *Permeability* and *Accessibility*). These qualities of the built environment support the human scale and slower speed of pedestrian movement. The mixed land use enhances compactness through living and working in the same localised community, leading to diversity and affordability. Infrastructure patterns can increase positive pedestrian experience through the width of streets, sidewalk size and quality, and support elements like benches and sitting areas. Other factors are streets integrated with green elements and public spaces such as urban squares and parks providing richness (see *Publicness*). Population density is important, as it provides a critical mass of people for retail to function and transit to run. Strong edge conditions also support walkability as they provide interactivity, visual interest through presence and rhythm, and a series of destinations along an axial path. There are many barriers to walkability. Some of these are dead end paths, cul-de-sacs, isolated or highly contained areas, high-speed movement corridors with minimal consideration for cross-movement patterns, and large blocks with little to no permeability.

While compactness is important for walkability, so too is connecting pedestrian mobility infrastructure to larger-scale mobility networks. This allows people to transition seamlessly from small-scale experiences to longer-distance mobility options. At a larger scale, walkability relates to the development of multiple centres across an urban area, which are strongly connected through these mobility networks (see *Node*). Walkability reduces dependency on energy-intensive modes of transport and provides a balanced infrastructure in terms of energy consumption. This allows communities greater flexibility in engaging resources and to be more sustainable in terms of continuity and adaptability of activities and experiences.

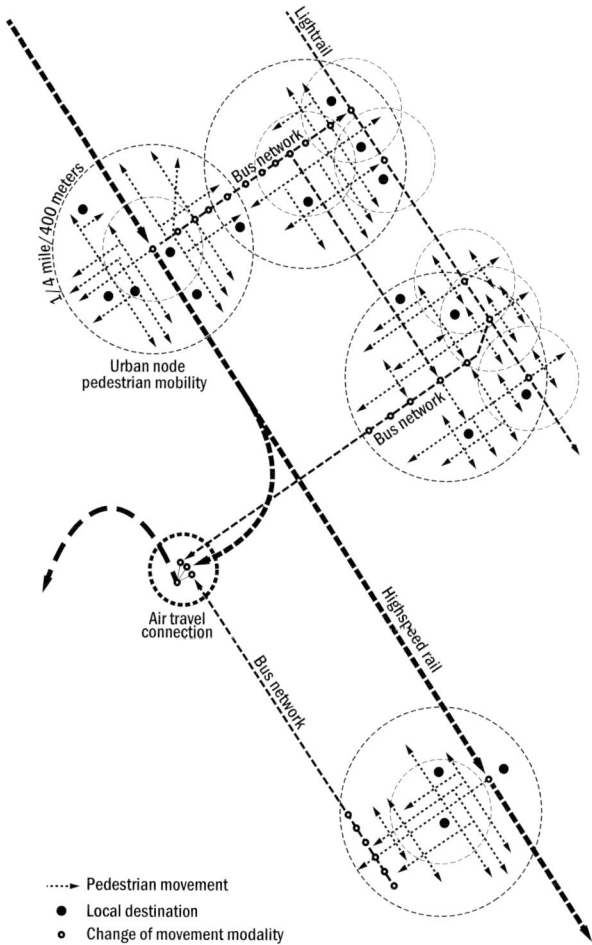

Light rail

1/4 mile / 400 meters

Bus network

Urban node
pedestrian mobility

Bus network

High speed rail

Air travel
connection

Bus network

┄┄► Pedestrian movement

● Local destination

○ Change of movement modality

EXTENDED mobility network

SOCIO-SPATIAL IDEAS

DOI: 10.4324/9781003254935-41

WE MIGHT NOT CONSIDER the space around us to be important. We often associate space with concepts such as background, emptiness, and neutrality. Our attention tends towards the making and placing of objects such as buildings, monuments, streetlights, and signs. However, our lives are spent in the space between these objects, and it is in these voids that we *build our relationships with other people*. Many of these relationships are spatialised, which situate human social values and relations within a particular configuration of the environment.

When humans gather together to live, work, play, and form a community, the spaces in which we associate are shaped through urban design to support the needs of those people. While many of these needs are physiological—about movement, visibility, and connection—many others are about more abstract concepts such as social organisation, belonging, networks, accessibility, and varying degrees of attention. All of these experiences are affected by the organisation and configuration of our urban spaces. When urban designers link types of land use to movement infrastructure and reinforce each through public gathering areas such as urban squares or parks, the resultant experience is social rather than formal. However, the desired social interactions would not be as successful without the supporting formal composition. This section addresses ideas focusing on the relation of one bounded space to another, the potential for social interaction, and the meaning that is created when experienced. The ideas use aspects from formal concepts and situated notions, but the focus shifts from movement, object, and void relationships to more complex human interaction through fundamental social expectations.

ACCESSIBILITY

ACCESSIBILITY IS THE CAPACITY to see, understand, move, engage, or use something without barrier or hindrance. It is a quality or a distinctive characteristic of a thing, space, or entity. In urban design, accessibility refers to how easily a space can be seen and accessed. Once in a space, accessibility refers to how easily a wide range of people can engage in the activities that space was intended to support (see *Diversity*).

Visual accessibility is defined by how clearly one part of an urban space can be seen from another. The degree of visual accessibility is often controlled by sightlines between spaces as well as by urban edges or street-walls (see *Edge* and *Visibility*). Street-walls can increase visual accessibility through the placement and scale of windows, degree of transparency of openings, and connecting interior activities to exterior spaces. Visual accessibility, in conjunction with physical accessibility, is critical for public experience in the city, specifically in terms of pedestrian activities and movement.

Physical accessibility is dependent on the arrangement of elements in the city. A major factor of that arrangement is the design of the urban grid, how it defines urban grain (see *Grain*) and allows or restricts different types of movement (see *Mobility*). A high degree of physical accessibility depends on supporting an ease of movement through providing multiple routes between spaces, including the possibility of choice, opportunities, and flexibility of paths. The reduction of restrictions and limitations on movement is also important. Urban space with a fine grain, small block structure, and continuous grid has high accessibility, because it offers greater choices of routes to go from one part to another part in the urban environment with fewer interruptions in terms of physical barriers and change in mode of movement.

Grid permeability and urban grain together impact a comprehensive public experience in places through visual and physical accessibility (see

DOI: 10.4324/9781003254935-42

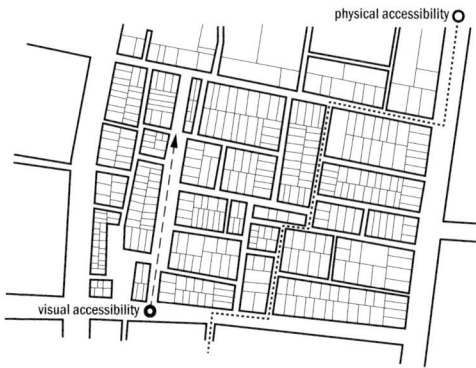

High permeability and grain with high accessibility

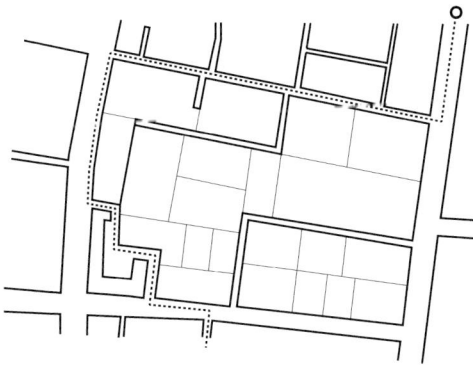

Low permeability and grain with low accessibility

Accessibility through PERMEABILITY and GRAIN

Publicness). This means that accessible urban areas should support desired and intended use both spatially and socially. The opposite can also be important, and accessibility sometimes requires the restriction of undesirable and unintended use (see *Use*). Accessibility determines how people can enter, engage, experience, and leave public spaces like streets, parks, squares, and alleys through the configuration of paths. Greater accessibility or ease with which we can get somewhere increases the probability we meet someone, and hence opportunities of exchange of information and interaction—properties of publicness in spaces. An accessible street or neighbourhood is typically more active than a less accessible street or neighbourhood. There are more people on the street, more activities co-existing and a higher possibility of engagement between those people and activities (see *Co-Awareness*).

Accessibility varies across urban scales and we often distinguish the accessibility at the city scale from accessibility at a local scale. Accessibility on a city scale refers to how easy or difficult it is to go from one place to all other places in the city. This scale of accessibility helps us understand how a city is connected and integrated. Local accessibility refers to the spatial integration within an area that supports engagement between people through interaction, exchange, and gathering (see *Connectedness*). Good accessibility at both city and local scales provides more opportunities for social interaction through increasing ease of movement and visibility. This makes good accessibility a desired quality for any urban zone that thrives through increasing pedestrian and vehicular movement such as retail and commercial zones.

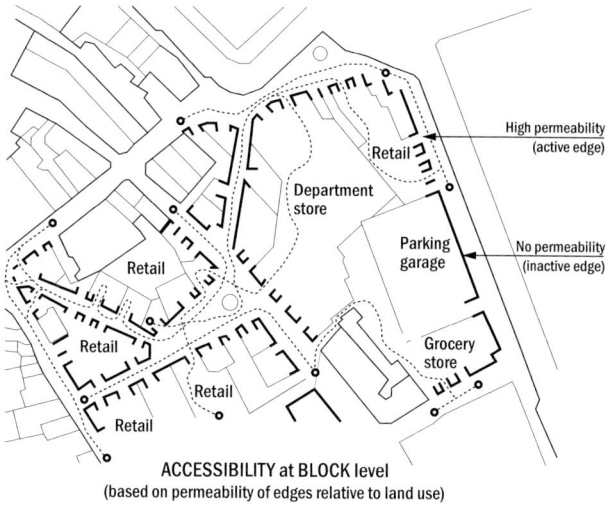

High permeability (active edge)

No permeability (inactive edge)

Retail

Department store

Parking garage

Grocery store

Retail

Retail

Retail

Retail

ACCESSIBILITY at BLOCK level
(based on permeability of edges relative to land use)

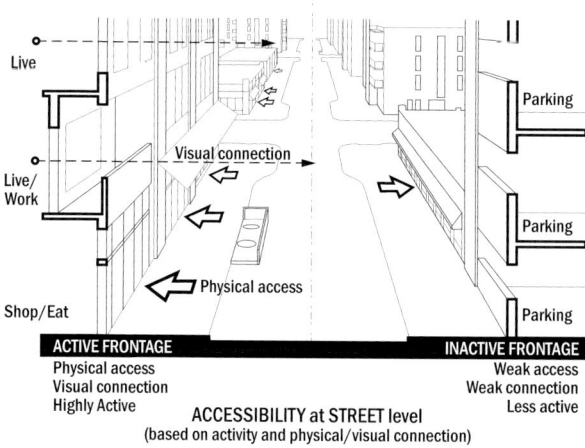

Live

Live/ Work

Shop/Eat

Visual connection

Physical access

Parking

Parking

Parking

ACTIVE FRONTAGE
Physical access
Visual connection
Highly Active

INACTIVE FRONTAGE
Weak access
Weak connection
Less active

ACCESSIBILITY at STREET level
(based on activity and physical/visual connection)

Accessibility and PERMEABILITY

ACTIVATION

ACTIVATION OCCURS WHEN a thing is in operation. We often think about this idea in terms of two states—either something is 'on' or it is 'off'. While we can consider how a powered object is activated by pressing a button or flipping a switch, the concept also applies to other entities, spaces, events, and ideas. If we had a vase on a table without holding anything, then that vase is inactive. An empty vase is in an off position and not in operation as it is not performing as it was intended. However, if we place some flowers into the vase, we have now activated the vase. Likewise, an activated person is one who is motivated to move and act. An activated idea is one that is put into operation to affect the world. An activated space is a location that is used as fully as possible. In all these cases, the thing that is activated performs as intended and to its fullest extent.

In urban design, we consider a space that is full of human interactions and events as vibrant and, thus, activated. The interaction increases the perceived quality of an area through adding interest and a sense of life. Activation of space occurs by allowing planned events (see *Use*) to be engaged through movement infrastructure, often leading to spontaneous interactions (see *Connectedness*). Urban forms that have a higher degree of exposure and support higher levels of possible engagement will tend toward more activation (see *Edge* and *Accessibility*). Activation needs a critical mass of activities that supports interaction, fosters healthy social settings, provides a feeling of safety and security, and encourages people to engage with the extensive amenities.

Urban activation is usually associated with public spaces (see *Publicness*). These operate as gathering areas and desirable paths and destinations linked to population density sources such as residential areas (see *Node* and *Path*). One of the most common engaging spaces is an activated frontage with social activities such as retail and cultural events or places

DOI: 10.4324/9781003254935-43

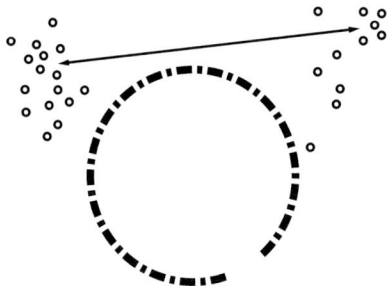

PASSIVE container

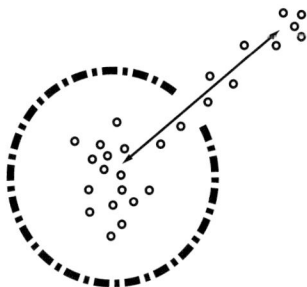

ACTIVE container

for meeting and gathering (see *Frontage*). Active frontages rely on fine urban grain, creating a vertical rhythm to the street and often combined with lively internal uses and events visible from outside, or ones that spill onto the street (see *Grain*, *Rhyme*, and *Rhythm*). This pattern is important for activated spaces as well as activated frontages, as it introduces a large range of different activities on an edge or within a block (see *Diversity*). These activities are supported by frequent openings like doors for physical access and windows for visual access (see *Interest*). Views of the indoor activities create opportunities for making the land uses apparent and provide interest to the passers-by. They also allow interaction among residents and visitors through visual access as well as contribute to comfort and safety of being in an active urban area (see *Visibility*). Frontage has a direct relationship with the perceived quality of a street and a neighbourhood. Its activation directly relates to interest, life, and vitality of the public realm (see *Identity*).

Many things can work against making activated space perform as it was intended. At a district or city scale, an edge, a node, or a corridor might be passive through low connectivity and permeability. Neighbourhood spaces might be inaccessible through lack of visibility or connections through paths. At the block or street scale, the frontage might be passive through a large block of blank walls with few points of physical or visual access.

Small blocks

○ Physical access
····· Movement

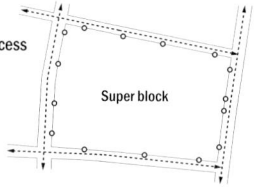

Super block

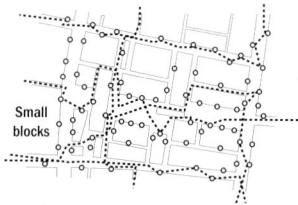

More permeable, highly active

Less permeable, highly passive

Street activation — PATH and PERMEABILITY

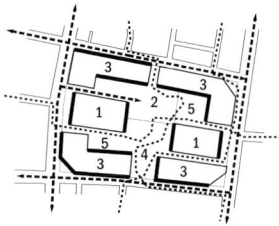

1. Retail
2. Parking
3. Residence
4. Plaza
5. Courtyard
····· Pedestrian
---► Vehicular
━━━ Active frontage

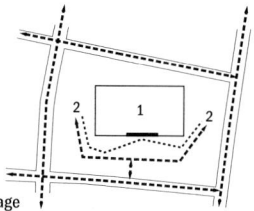

Mix of uses, highly active

Single use, highly passive

Block activation — EVENTS and MASSING CONFIGURATION

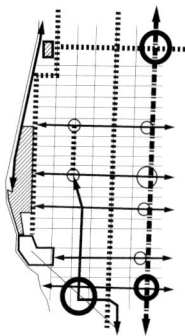

⬤ Gateway
○ Node
▨ Destination
······· Retail boulevard
◄─► Greenway
◄━━► Lightrail
◄╍╍► Highway

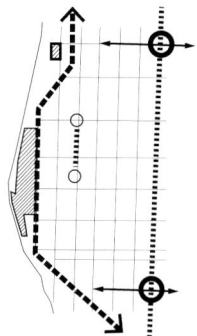

Node & infrastructure network,
highly active

Isolated node & infrastructure,
highly passive

District activation — infrastructure CONNECTIONS and Destination PROXIMITY

Range of activation in STREET, BLOCK, and DISTRICT

COHERENCE

COHERENCE IS PRESENT WHEN SEVERAL ELEMENTS are interpreted to align towards a single objective, goal, or focus. This can be a physical space, event, quality, or idea. People use coherence to make sense of complexity by understanding how the parts of something might relate to each other and how they support a greater whole. When things share a common relationship towards a perceived goal, it increases legibility of that context, situation, or experience by making it easier for us to understand. As a judgement, coherence in a context or situation is considered to be very positive, as it aligns with our notion of truth (see *Authenticity*). It also relates to the human desire for sense-making through balance, order, and pattern (see *Balance* and *Pattern*). In urban design, coherence occurs primarily in two ways. First, *formal coherence* is present in the interpreted relationships between objects. It includes buildings and infrastructure, their physical characteristics, and spatial relationships. Second, *event coherence* occurs when the activities, occupancies, and experiences in a location are aligned and make sense.

Formal coherence is the basis of the legibility of the built environment and supports our ability to understand, and thus navigate, that environment efficiently. A coherent environment is one that can be broken into smaller, easily understood elements while also maintaining the relationship of those elements back to the overall environment. Generally, it is one that is tightly connected, close, and composed of known ordering principles (see *Axis*, *Centre*, *Grid*, and *Node*). Ordering principles are used as a guide to align elements within the environment. They also create predictability as they allow us to understand what we might expect, even in a location where we have not yet been. For example, an urban grid is a coherent pattern when all the parts of the environment reinforce the grid through building orientation, building massing, circulation patterns,

DOI: 10.4324/9781003254935-44

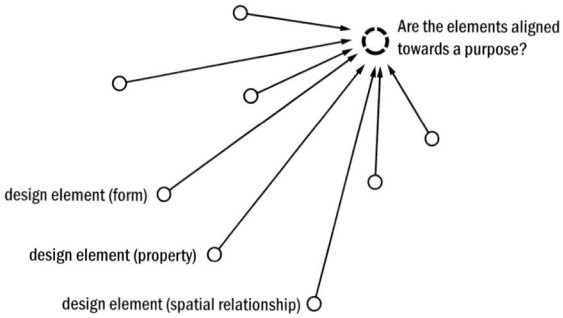

Are the elements aligned towards a purpose?

design element (form)

design element (property)

design element (spatial relationship)

Coherence through alignment of OBJECT and PURPOSE

and property setbacks. Once we understand that the grid organises space through repeated intersections, we can easily extend this idea to predict how to navigate to a destination we have not previously visited.

Event coherence, or functional coherence, occurs when all the activities in a space or location are aligned through characteristics or event affinities (see *MATBH: Event Affinity*). A coherent district, for example, can include many different types of occupancies and events, but they will all align with the overall identity of that district. A residential area is more understandable when planned occupancy types align with the idea of domesticity, leisure, and dwelling. Event coherence can also develop on an individual basis through experiences and memories. Our patterns of interaction can create familiarity through experience and degree of contact that allows a thing's identity and organisation to be clearly understood. For example, our own neighbourhood is always coherent to us, where familiarity and comfort have been gained through everyday use and rituals.

Cities are places of immense complexity across multiple scales. It is coherence that allows us to have legibility within this complexity. Without this understanding, it would be difficult to navigate, move through, and make sense of the urban environment. Coherence provides a conceptual and perceptual order based on the relationship between buildings at multiple urban scales as a representation of grain (see *Grain*) and connected to accessibility (see *Accessibility*). This basic human interpretation of our built environment allows us to thrive through organisation and sense-making. However, there are moments when breaking from coherence can be positive and used to enrich the experience of an environment (see *Interest*).

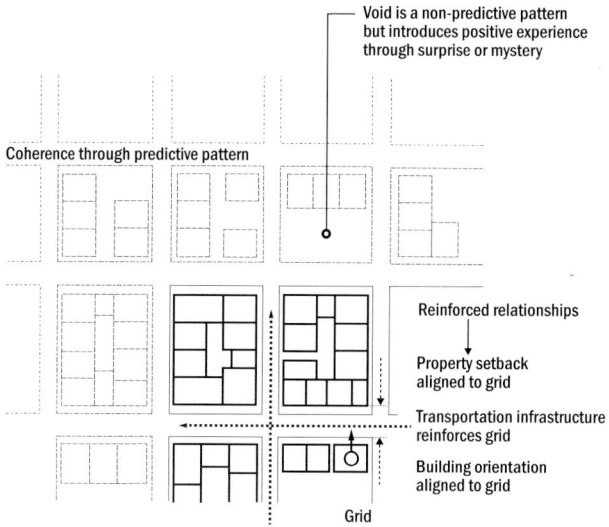

Void is a non-predictive pattern but introduces positive experience through surprise or mystery

Coherence through predictive pattern

Reinforced relationships

Property setback aligned to grid

Transportation infrastructure reinforces grid

Building orientation aligned to grid

Grid

Coherence through ORDERING PRINCIPLES

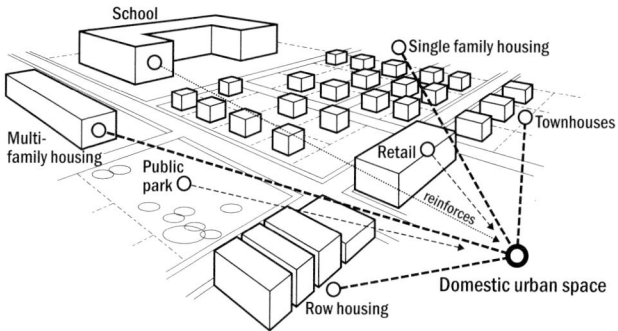

School

Single family housing

Townhouses

Multi-family housing

Public park

Retail

reinforces

Domestic urban space

Row housing

Coherence through EVENT AFFINITY

CONTROL

CONTROL IS A TYPE OF AGENCY IN WHICH a thing has the ability to make an action and the authority, capacity, and influence to make that action happen. The ability to move freely and act physically is one of the most fundamental forms of agency for humans. However, when that agency also includes the capacity for our actions to influence other things, it expresses control. In this way, control defines a central operational relationship between humans and our built environment. While the most common thing we control is ourselves, we also project the idea of control onto objects, events, and ideas. This includes allowing others to control us where the 'others' might be an inanimate object or an influential idea. When we shape the environment around us to suit our needs, we are expressing control. However, when we allow the environment to shape our actions and movements, we are ceding control to others.

In urban design, one type of control occurs through organising objects and spaces in the physical environment. When we interpret our surroundings, we use the physical characteristics and relative spatial location of things to determine what is important and how the pieces relate to one another. This system of importance allows us to understand and decide what matters in our surroundings (see *MATBH: Hierarchy*). For example, zoning sets up priorities by allowing certain things or qualities considered to be important in the community and to control or restrict other things considered less important. The most common physical expressions of control are based on relative scale, containment, proximity, axial extension, centrality, and increased vertical elevation through topography or massing. Control is often conceived as power over things within close physical distance, as proximity allows us the ability to make actions with our body (*MATBH: Proximity*). Scale also matters in these relationships, as we also understand that larger things tend to have

DOI: 10.4324/9781003254935-45

Decreased sense of
control with distance

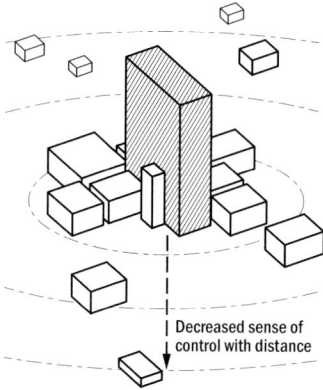

Large scale organizes smaller

SCALE and PROXIMITY

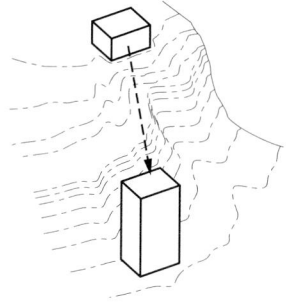

Higher dominates lower

ELEVATION

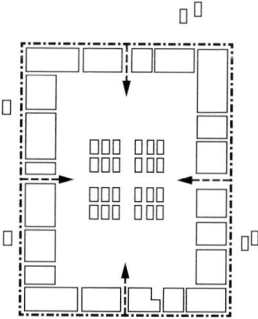

Outside edges project inwards
Boundary controls interior

CONTAINMENT

radial presence

area control

projected control

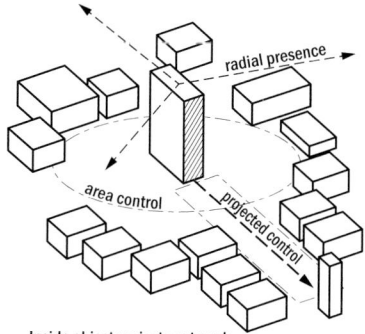

Inside object projects outwards
Centrality and axis dominate through extension

CENTRALITY and AXIAL EXTENSION

Control and SITUATED CHARACTERISTICS

physical power over smaller things. We also know that when one object or space surrounds another, the surrounding element restricts and affects the surrounded element (see *Containment*). Thus, large urban objects are generally understood as controlling smaller ones, a space with a strong boundary will control all that is within that container, and things taller or higher will tend to be seen as controlling things below them. This is why the bounding of space, with or without a centre, is important in order to define owned territory (see *Boundary* and *Capacity*) or how a land-mark gathers an area around itself to create a unique spatial identity (see *Landmark* and *Identity*).

A second type of control present in the urban environment is how the built environment offers certain options for physical and visual acces-sibility and interaction (see *Choice*). These affordances allow individuals within that environment to make choices based on options for occu-pying and moving through space (see *Use* and *Mobility*). The possible choices that our environment provides affects experiences at several scales. These range from restricting or supporting public interactions and privacy levels to controlling population densities, land use, and urban growth patterns. The available choices of path when moving from one space to another affects the experience of individuals in their own agency (see *Permeability*). In this sense, control is associated with immediate connections, intersections, nodes, visibility, and accessibility. Though con-trol is a strategic concept for development direction and a tool applied to decrease the range of possible outcomes, not all urban experiences benefit from tightly controlled environments with minimal options, while others are negatively impacted by too many choices leading to lack of cohesion, legibility, and identity.

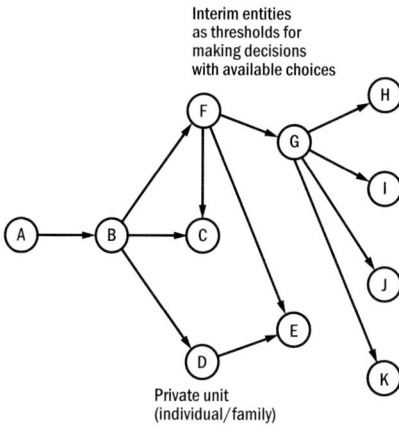

Interim entities
as thresholds for
making decisions
with available choices

Private unit
(individual/family)

Control of EXPERIENCE through MOVEMENT choices

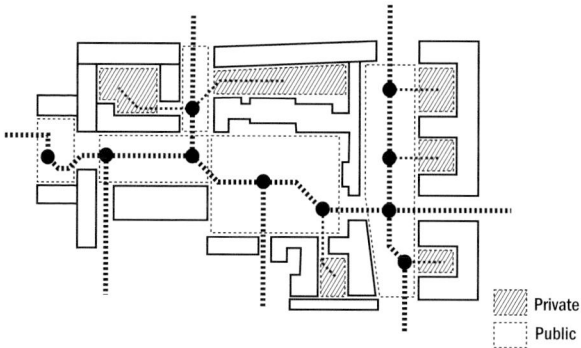

Private

Public

Control in ACCESS and PUBLICNESS

LOCALITY

LOCALITY IS A SPECIFIC POINT OF space and time where each of us exists. It is understood through the extension of our body into that space and what is immediately accessible to our senses (see *MATBH: Proximity*). Through the presence of our body and the associations with elements, objects, and people in the vicinity, one space becomes distinct from other locations. While locality starts with ourselves, we extend the same idea to objects and spaces around us (see *MATBH: Personification*). Locality, then, is the specific placement of a thing that makes one space identifiability different from another (see *Identity* and *Place*). That localised positioning includes the object itself and its relationship to other things in the same area through proximity and temporality. In this way, space becomes situated and distinct, with the object and its associated elements defining a boundary of influence.

In urban design, locality is created through physical characteristics of massing and open space (see *Figure-Ground* and *Grain*), types of events and activities supported by those physical forms (see *Use*), and systems of movement infrastructure reinforcing those relationships (see *Connectedness* and *Activation*). A locality occurs when these diverse elements are associated in a close network that defines a perceived boundary (see *Compactness*). Larger urban developments can also define their own locality if they are coherent and well-activated. An urban housing or retail corridor project creates its own local context through scale and influence, affecting the quality of space within and around it. Although the quality might change, all moments in the built environment produce a locality defined by its physical characteristics and its capacity to produce and influence distinct human experiences within a boundary.

DOI: 10.4324/9781003254935-46

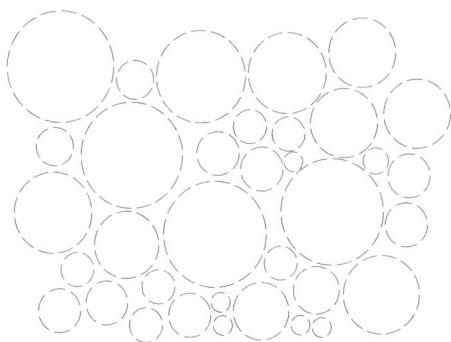

Space and objects as BOUNDED VOLUMES

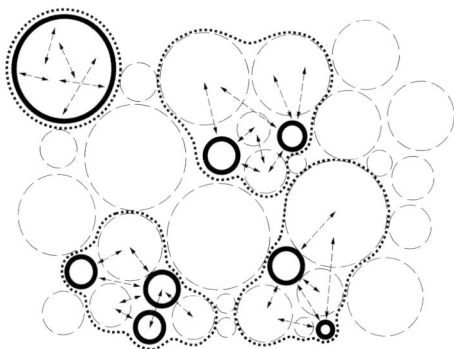

Locality as SITUATED VOLUMES with ASSOCIATIONS

PRESENCE

PRESENCE IS THE DEGREE OF AWARENESS and recognition of a thing in the vicinity of others within a context. It is based on the amount of attention we give something and how we interpret its impact on its environment. When something has a large presence, we are quite aware of that thing. Things with reduced presence are not as noticeable. When people have presence, they can influence the behaviour of other people around them. Objects with presence in their environments have the same ability to influence things around them and gain significance.

Visibility is the most common form of presence. If something is within our visual field, we are aware of its physical presence. As something attracts our gaze through its shape, surface characteristics, or positioning, it takes more of our attention. This attention creates a hierarchy of importance in how we engage the world around us (see *MATBH: Hierarchy*). Something with a presence can be used to organise other elements around it (see *MATBH: Importance*). They are understood to project outwards from their visible surfaces into the surrounding area. The stronger the sense of projection, the stronger the perceived presence and the larger the effect on the surrounding environment. While visibility is a primary source of information from our environment, all our senses have the capacity to make us aware of something. We might also hear a sound or catch a smell that catches our attention. Where visual presence might be fixed, sound and smell are often temporal or periodic.

In urban design, presence can operate through radial or axial visibility (see *Visibility*). Radial presence occurs when an urban object or space extends its effect in several directions but without a particular focus. These elements tend to be larger in scale relative to the surrounding context. Significant buildings, infrastructural objects like a bridge or tower, or natural features such as a mountain or cliff operate as moments of radial

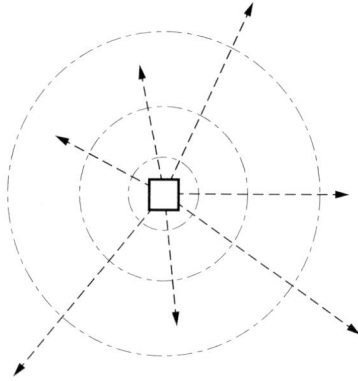

RADIAL presence

AXIAL presence

presence (see *Landmark*). An axial presence is the extension of the urban object or space along a line of projected axis or as a point of terminated vista. This is focused in one direction generally using presence as a focus point. Both types of presence are connected to moments in the environment that organise our experiences, affecting how we understand that urban context.

While urban objects can have presence through formal characteristics related to our senses, it is also possible to have event presence in urban spaces. Events are temporary or periodic presences that occur within physical environments. These might be time-based activities supported by urban form and containment such as markets, celebrations, and civic gatherings. We might notice an event's presence through visual expressions of activity density though it is just as likely to have presence through sound as the primary sensory information.

Most of our urban context works as a background for our lives, in which not all aspects need to have a high degree of presence. Some locations and landmarks do require a larger degree of contrast and difference from their surroundings to operate as organising elements and to create sensibility (see *Figure-Ground* and *Coherence*). A legible urban context consists of situated patterns of rhyme or rhythm, involving elements with less variation and contrast in their presence as they use similarity and repetition (see *MATBH: Similarity* and *MATBH: Repetition*). This hierarchy of presence with large similarity and a few distinctions create a balanced urban experience.

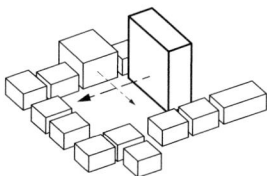

Difference creates hierarchy of presence

POINT presence

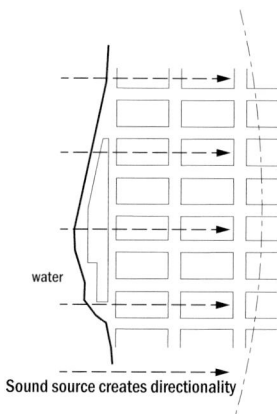

water

Sound source creates directionality

FIELD presence

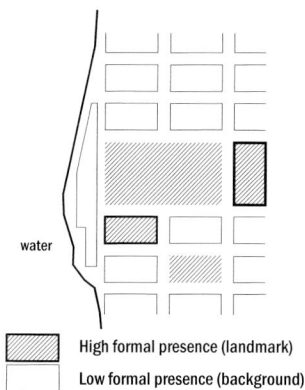

water

▨	High formal presence (landmark)
☐	Low formal presence (background)

FORMAL presence — fixed

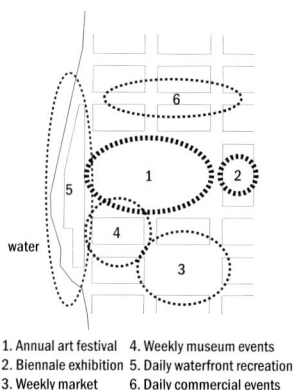

water

1. Annual art festival   4. Weekly museum events
2. Biennale exhibition   5. Daily waterfront recreation
3. Weekly market   6. Daily commercial events

EVENT presence — temporal

URBAN presence

PUBLICNESS

PUBLICNESS IS AN EXPERIENCE OF social contexts in which moments of co-awareness can support various types of human-to-human interactions (see *Co-Awareness*). In situations of publicness, an individual gives up some control over their body and their environment in order to receive some benefit. Notions of publicness extend into the idea of public life where social activity occurs in accessible spaces that support inter-action between people through observation or engagement. Public life is generally directed towards some common benefit through a shared community. In contrast, privacy consists of moments of intimacy and self-involvement created through limiting access to our bodies—spaces and situations where we decide who and what might affect us (see *MATBH: Privacy*).

We often think of publicness and privacy as two discrete opposite states, but these concepts are really two ends of a gradient. In the case of the physical environment, most spaces are neither fully public nor entirely private but somewhere between the two. For urban design, significant pri-ority is given towards the publicness side of the gradient. This is due to a focus on developing infrastructure and development patterns for large volumes of people rather than designing only for individuals. Publicness is also based on shared spaces that tolerate different interests and behaviours of diverse groups of people. The identity of these spaces transcends the individual and reinforces a shared belonging (see *Character*).

The basis of publicness is accessibility and equitable experience (see *Balance*). Accessibility is achieved through the spatial composition of the urban environments using the primary human experiences of visi-bility (see *Co-Awareness* and *Visibility*) and movement (see *Mobility* and *Connectedness*). When two or more people can see each other, it creates the possibility of a relationship between them. In order to extend that

DOI: 10.4324/9781003254935-48

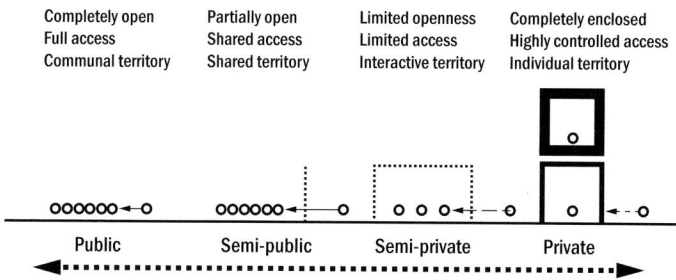

| Completely open
Full access
Communal territory | Partially open
Shared access
Shared territory | Limited openness
Limited access
Interactive territory | Completely enclosed
Highly controlled access
Individual territory |

Public   Semi-public   Semi-private   Private

Gradient of PUBLICNESS

mutual relationship from sight to activity, we need to create an adjacency through decreasing physical distance. This requires physical accessibility through ease of movement and greater connectedness. In urban spaces, it is the physical organisation and configuration of objects (i.e., buildings, monuments, signs) and spaces (i.e., streets, parks, squares, plazas) that influence how people might see, move, engage with one another, and experience the environment around them through their senses. A public space supports visual access from various points of view (see *Permeability*). Entrance locations, emphasis on street presence and frontage, and visual clues for interaction offer greater opportunities for co-presence and co-awareness that also lead to publicness. Spaces along the city's movement pattern allow greater potential for natural movement and more opportunities for attraction of activities and interactions. This mobility and attraction lend greater potential of density of use and activities. The combination of sight and motion then suggests the possibilities to how people gather and how they might interact (see *Centre*).

An important aspect for both physical and visual accessibility in public space is the threshold (see *MATBH: Threshold*). Thresholds are transitions, like gateways, colonnades, and arcades, which become decision points for choices and access to public spaces (see *Choice*). Obvious and hard thresholds like doors and gates could be detrimental to publicness and result in less availability and more individual control of public spaces. On the other hand, subtle thresholds like arcades and colonnades or porches, entrance courts, and loggias can provide significant entrance conditions and useful information about public space through change in scale and material.

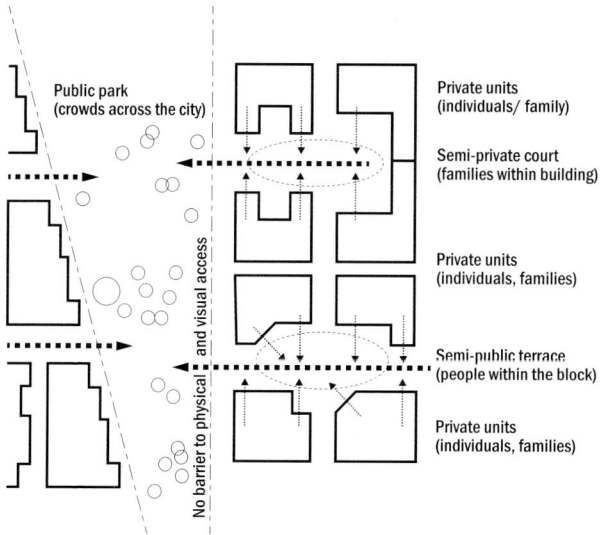

Public park
(crowds across the city)

Private units
(individuals/ family)

Semi-private court
(families within building)

Private units
(individuals, families)

Semi-public terrace
(people within the block)

Private units
(individuals, families)

No barrier to physical and visual access

Publicness gradient based on MOVEMENT and GATHERING

RESILIENCE

RESILIENCE IS THE ABILITY OF SOMETHING to return to its previous state after an event that introduces stress. We understand this event as a force which might be short and intense or long and persistent (see *MATBH: Force*). If something introduces a dynamic action to something else, such as bending, compression, penetration, pressure, pushing, or twisting, we expect some response. This might be for the thing acted upon to move, fall over, crumple, or collapse. Once the force has been removed, the question is, what happens next? If that thing that was acted upon was resilient, it would return to its previous position, location, activity, or operation regardless of the effect of the stress. Although this is a physical experience, we use the same idea to understand more complex and abstract concepts.

In a human context, resilience is the capacity to adapt and recover so as to sustain safety and security in a complex and dynamic environment. Urban resilience addresses the physical infrastructure and urban massing to continue to provide social services and to support enriched human lives after the introduction and removal of a dramatic force. Forces that affect urban systems can be environmental, economic, and social. Environmental forces are dramatic climatic changes and extreme weather events such as hurricanes, tornados, blizzards, floods, wildfire, drought, ice storms, dust storms, and hailstorms. Economic forces are things such as disinvestment of resources, economic decline, unemployment, real estate foreclosures, and bankruptcy. Social forces include events such as segregation and displacement, population decline, social unrest and riots, and loss of publicness and physical access to shared spaces (see *Segregation*, *Publicness*, and *Accessibility*). Each of these puts stress on our urban habitat, commerce, energy, food, and water infrastructure systems, which affects the quality of life for inhabitants in urban areas. Each urban system also has a limit of what it can provide or support (see *Capacity*). A dynamic force

DOI: 10.4324/9781003254935-49

Stress as force

Application of force
Deformation of a thing

Removal of force
Continued failure of a thing

Non-resiliency

Stress as force

Application of force
Deformation of a thing

Removal of force
Recovery of a thing

Resiliency

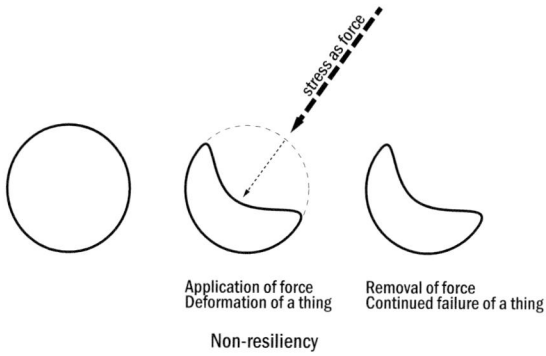

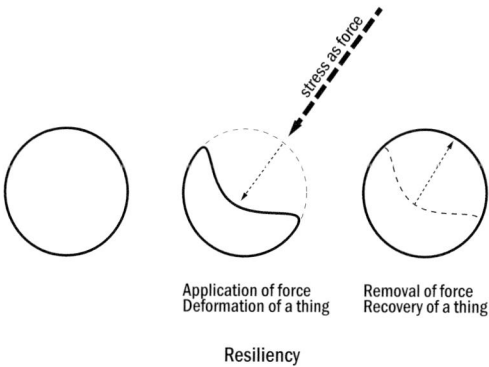

Resilience versus non-resilience in DEFORMATION

that exceeds that limit will put the urban system under stress. A resilient urban system is one that reduces loss of form and physical infrastructure once the stress has been managed or removed.

Resilience as a design idea is about understanding vulnerabilities in the urban environment and then designing to minimise those weaknesses. It is also about the ability of urban systems to maintain functionality during as well as after stress (see *Stability*). Vulnerability occurs through reduced physical and service capacity as well as loss of diversity, identity, and the sense of place (see *Diversity* and *Place*). These affect the ability of an urban space to provide for the needs of people in a way that is robust, healthy, and sustainable. However, designing for resilience does not mean to make an environment static and unchanging. The response to a force often requires an urban environment to be flexible or adaptable to changes in population density, technology, mobility, or environmental events. This might mean that urban forms, services, or infrastructure are designed with redundancies or flexibility to changes. Urban areas with multiple compact centres support high density while reducing the sense of overcrowding work towards resiliency, as each centre is highly independent but still strongly connected to each other (see *Connectedness*, *Mobility*, and *Choice*). Zoning and land use can also support resilient urban spaces when their distribution and organisation allow for diversity of occupants and events, including supporting a wide range of housing types, economic and family structures, mixed-use types, temporary activities, and changes in mobility patterns and types (see *Diversity*).

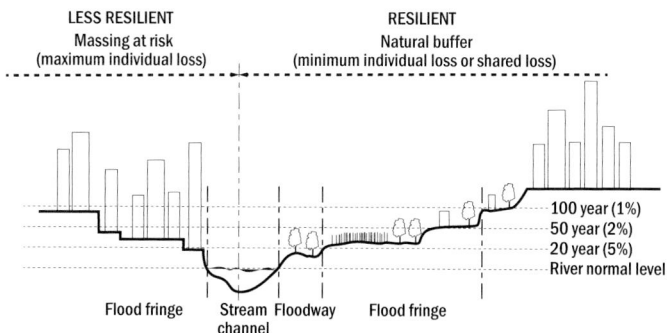

LESS RESILIENT
Massing at risk
(maximum individual loss)

RESILIENT
Natural buffer
(minimum individual loss or shared loss)

100 year (1%)
50 year (2%)
20 year (5%)
River normal level

Flood fringe   Stream   Floodway   Flood fringe
                      channel

Resilience from ENVIRONMENTAL STRESS

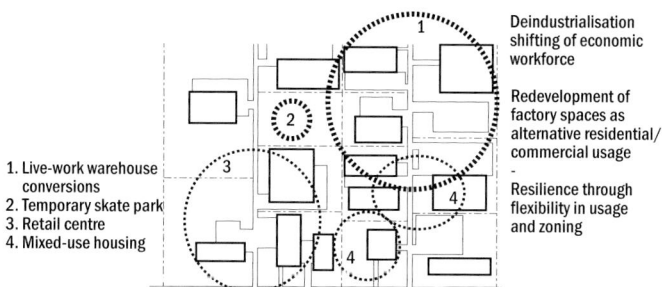

1

Deindustrialisation
shifting of economic
workforce

Redevelopment of
factory spaces as
alternative residential/
commercial usage
-
Resilience through
flexibility in usage
and zoning

1. Live-work warehouse
   conversions
2. Temporary skate park
3. Retail centre
4. Mixed-use housing

Resilience from ECONOMIC STRESS

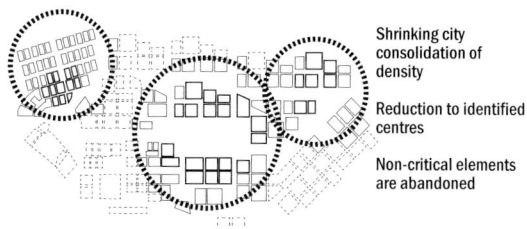

Shrinking city
consolidation of
density

Reduction to identified
centres

Non-critical elements
are abandoned

Resilience from SOCIAL STRESS

SENSIBILITY

SENSIBILITY IS THE PROCESS OF organising knowledge gathered through our senses to understand the complex and dynamic world around us. Human thinking involves a circular relationship between our mind, body, and environment in which our senses are a primary source of experience. Humans receive information through visibility, movement, and balance followed by sound, smell, touch, and taste. When something is sensible, it is easily understandable because it is aligned with the way we interpret events and objects through these sensory inputs. This is why when we understand something, we call it 'making sense of that thing'. A sensible thing is something with which we can interact in human terms.

Urban sensibility is how the built environment is organised in a meaningful way for people. It is based on how we understand the organisation of materiality, massing, grain, and open space (see *Axis*, *Figure-Ground*, and *Grid*). The primary purpose of a sensible environment is to help people make sense of where they are and how to get to where they want to go (see *Legibility*). This ability to process information from our surroundings and navigate our environment is called wayfinding.

Wayfinding uses past and present information gathered by our senses in an environment to make decisions about location, direction, distance, and achieving spatial goals such as arriving at a location. It is supported by coherence and legibility of movement networks (see *Path*, *Connectedness*, and *Coherence*) and features that create recognisable patterns or differences (see *Pattern*). These complex patterns of information are organised conceptually as spatial processes, such as cognitive maps and route planning.

Cognitive maps are mental images of the relationship between places using cues from all our senses, which allow us to make short-term decisions to navigate to goals. They are grid based and expand in all directions, but they tend to support local and immediate sensibility needs. Cognitive

DOI: 10.4324/9781003254935-50

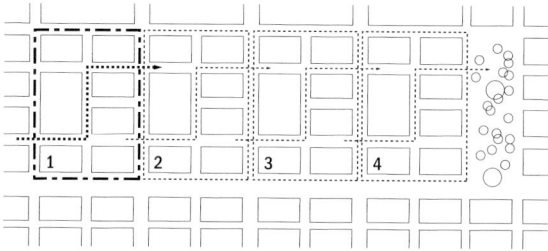

Understanding one location allows knowledge of other locations through similarity

Sensibility by PATTERNS

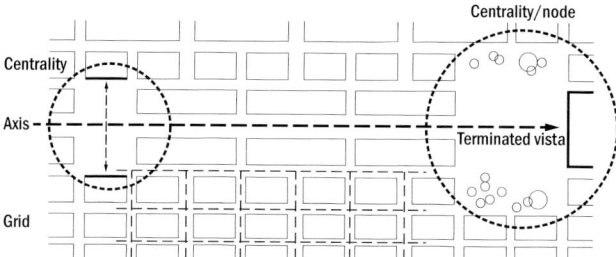

Understanding the environment through axis, centrality, radiosity and grid

Sensibility by ORDERING SYSTEMS

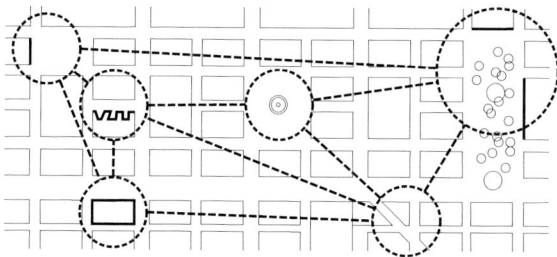

Understanding one location relation to other locations through difference

Sensibility by DIFFERENTIATION

maps use spatial memory, which is remembering locations of things and events in space and time. Things might be physical objects like landmarks with local or distant presence but could also be based on other sensory information such as smell or sound (see *Landmark* and *Presence*). Events might be everyday rituals or periodic occurrences in public places like bus stops, streets, markets, parks, or plazas. The mapping associates these things and events with one another, creating an imprecise memory of how space around us is organised. Cognitive maps are not explicit maps but layers of partial and vague associations of elements to help position ourselves in space. Physical characteristics of urban space can help or interfere with this process of cognitive mapping through high or low sensibility.

More refined and precise navigation uses route planning rather than cognitive maps. Route planning is a series of locations that are to be followed sequentially. As we arrive at one location, we interpret our surroundings for choices to identify and map a path to the next location in the sequence. This constant process of information collection, evaluation, interpretation, and decision making continues until we arrive at our final goal. The common urban element used for route planning is the node as an intersection of paths (see *Node*). It is at this point that a choice needs to be made, and we understand that our current location is an aspect of a larger, connected network.

Sensibility allows better communication and interaction between people and their environment. Sensible environments reinforce the ability to create consistent patterns of spatial moments of interest relating legibility to spatial memory. These mappable characteristics offer valuable elements for liveability, making sensibility a component of urban sustainability.

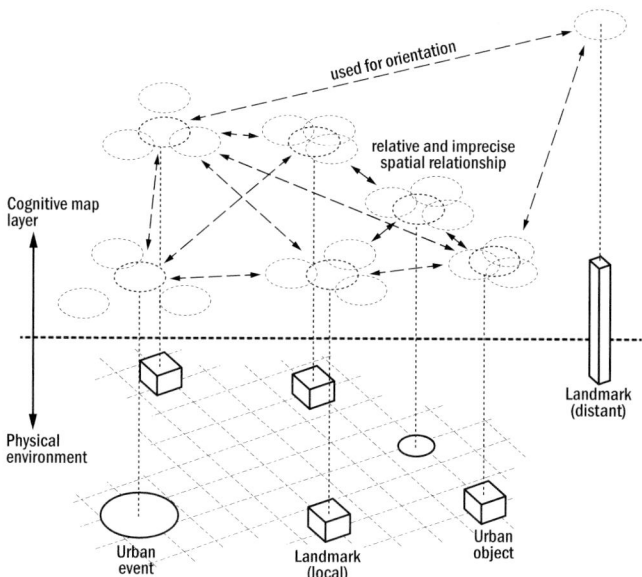

used for orientation

relative and imprecise
spatial relationship

Cognitive map
layer

Physical
environment

Landmark
(distant)

Urban
event

Landmark
(local)

Urban
object

Sensibility by COGNITIVE MAPPING

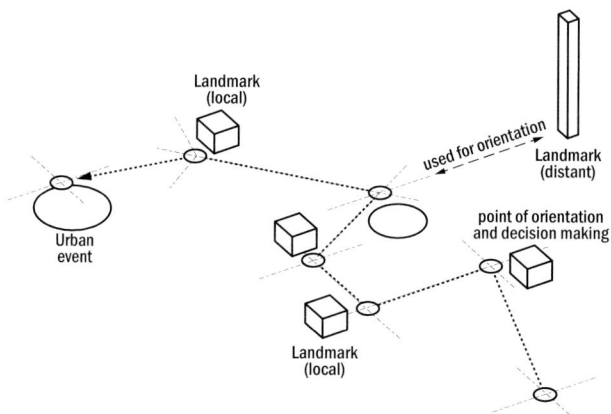

Landmark
(local)

used for orientation

Landmark
(distant)

Urban
event

point of orientation
and decision making

Landmark
(local)

Sensibility by ROUTE PLANNING

SEPARATION

SEPARATION OCCURS WHEN TWO THINGS are moved away from each other's presence and awareness. It is an act of isolation through suppression of an existing or possible relationship. A primary way in which those relationships are created is through physical proximity and visual alignment (see *Co-Awareness*, *Co-Presence*, and *MATBH: Relationship*). When those relationships are hindered through distance, open space, or intervening objects, we create separation. Separation is a socio-spatial idea which decreases awareness, presence, and attention that then eliminates opportunities for social interaction. There are both positive and negative aspects to separation.

When activities or events taking place in adjacent spaces are compatible with each other, they do not interfere and may even improve the experience (see *MATBH: Event Affinity*). However, when the presence of an activity causes conflict and decreased success for all adjacent events, this creates a negative event affinity. Separation is one response to negative event affinity when the proximity of events in one space is disturbing the success of an adjacent space. One way to mediate between conflicts is by moving the two events far apart. If we cannot separate events through distance, then some type of formal intervention is needed to negotiate the relationship between events in adjacent spaces. This might be a strong physical boundary such as a wall or the use of topography as a buffer to reduce the interaction between two areas. In urban design, a negative event or land use is often separated from other areas through policy regulation like zoning (see *Use*). For example, moving a chemical factory that emits noxious fumes and chemicals away from a residential area or waterfront is desirable for the safety and security of human life.

When separation is enforced by others and applied at a social level to adversely impact certain sections of the community, it becomes either

DOI: 10.4324/9781003254935-51

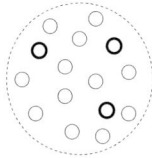

Inclusive

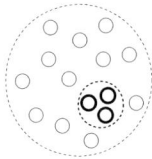

Integrated

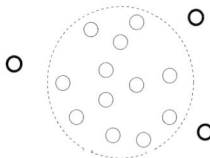

Excluded

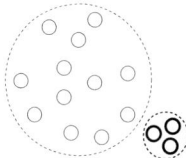

Segregated

FORMAL RELATIONSHIPS in separation

exclusion or segregation. Exclusion is isolation through the denial of activities. Segregation is isolation to perform those or similar activities but with physical and social separation from others of the same kind. The spatial effects of segregation are played out through the use of boundary, distance, and adjacency to create, control, and maintain certain separation where parts of a larger whole are treated differently (see *Boundary* and *Containment*). Any act of isolation between like elements with the intention to create unequal access is an act of segregation.

Urban segregation is a negative socio-spatial phenomenon that decreases the quality of the physical environment. It limits social experiences through restricting access and movement to spaces and resources, reducing specific opportunities (see *Permeability*, *Diversity*, and *Choice*). The effects can be found at multiple scales from street to district. In all cases, segregation affects the composition of social space in which people gather, form relationships, and obtain opportunities through interaction (see *Publicness*). The spatial effect of segregation is the regulation of access as well as a reduction in connections (see *Connectedness* and *Control*). The physical manifestation can be both explicit and implicit. Examples of explicit forms of segregation are a wall separating two neighbourhoods, a fenced park, or a plaza surrounded only by high-value residences. Implicit and more subtle segregation can occur through policies such as restricting public transportation, something that privileges those who can afford personal transportation. Similarly, zoning codes allowing only single-family residences implicitly exclude populations with less economic capacity, as they depend on shared housing and multifamily residential models.

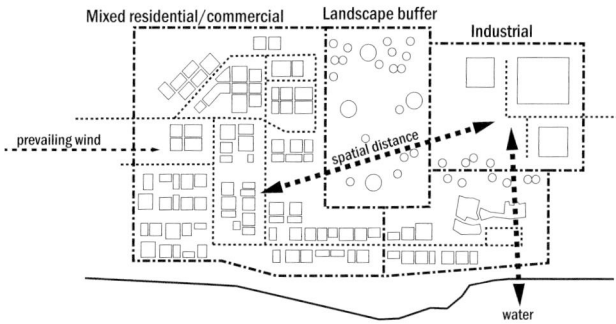

Separation to eliminate NEGATIVE EVENT AFFINITY

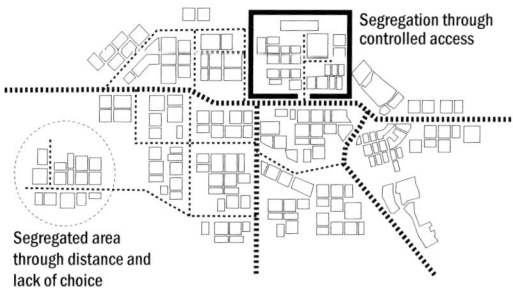

Segregation through DISTANCE, CHOICE, and ACCESS

STABILITY

STABILITY IS A CONDITION OF EQUILIBRIUM, where something is neither improving nor deteriorating. Our understanding of stability comes from our bodies and our sense of balance (see *Balance*). We are stable when we can maintain our upright posture against gravity and move without falling over. To do this, our muscles are constantly shifting in small ways, even if we are not actively aware of this process. We are not static, but we are stable through these small changes and in response to expected forces. Only when a force interacts with us unexpectedly, such as the ground moves suddenly or something knocks into us, is our stability put at risk. At this point, we attempt to return to a previous condition through shifting from unconscious interactions to conscious awareness. When something is stable through its ability to counteract internal and external forces and is able to react to expected and unexpected changes, we consider that thing to be sustainable (see *Capacity* and *Resilience*).

Urban stability is the ability of our built environment to support the fundamental needs and services of inhabitants of a community while under stress in both long and short time periods. The primary types of performative balance we find in urban design are environmental, social, economic, and infrastructural stability. While many of these factors are large-scale, complex, and involve interactions between many systems, they are also spatialised. This means that these issues depend on spatial positioning and human choices such as adjacency, boundary, accessibility, and materiality.

Environmental stability refers to any factor related to the relationship between people and the natural environment. This includes issues of biodiversity, energy and material balance, carbon sequestration, air, water, and soil quality, microclimate creation, and factors of pollution. The choice to apply a growth boundary, the introduction of tree canopies to control heat island effects, or an approach that minimises impermeable surfaces

DOI: 10.4324/9781003254935-52

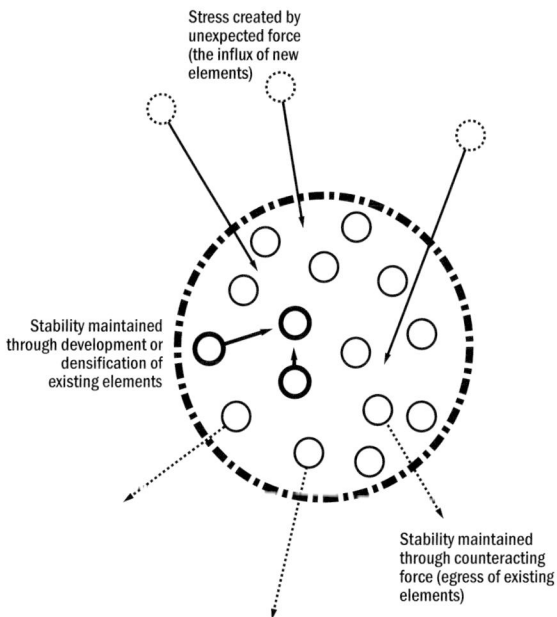

Stress created by
unexpected force
(the influx of new
elements)

Stability maintained
through development or
densification of
existing elements

Stability maintained
through counteracting
force (egress of existing
elements)

Stability through EQUILIBRIUM

to water are aspects of environmental stability (see *Expansion*). Social stability is related to issues between various groups of people. These involve supporting demographic changes that include issues of ageing, changes in lifestyle needs, safety, and security. Stability is closely connected to diversity in available choices of living (see *Diversity*). As people age in communities, their needs change along with physical abilities, health, family structure, activities, and social networks. A diversity of choices in built form, open space, events, and services, supporting varied and changing needs of its population, is critical to maintain a stable population. Economic stability is how the urban environment supports the relationship between people and finances. Accessibility and adjacency of people to work opportunities affects the financial health of individuals. Urban economic factors include reliability and efficiency of transportation networks, costs of living, and zoning patterns (see *Mobility, Separation, Use,* and *Choice*). Infrastructure stability is the capacity of an area to support its population over time through access to power, nutrition, mobility, waste management, and communication resources. Strongly connected areas with a diversity of options offer good stability.

Stability can be considered through balancing inputs and outputs. A long-term stable urban environment should balance between ease of accessibility of things coming into that space (attracting food, water, products, people) as compared to things leaving that space (exporting resources, waste, pollution, people). We can ask questions to examine urban sustainability, such as: How do we access a stable supply of water while managing our waste output? Or, how do we balance natural and human systems so they support rather than harm each other?

STRESS   COUNTERACTION   URBAN RESPONSE

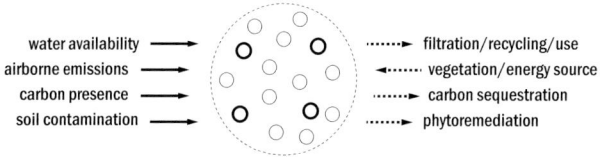

water availability →   ┈┈▶ filtration/recycling/use
airborne emissions →   ◀┈┈ vegetation/energy source
carbon presence →   ┈┈▶ carbon sequestration
soil contamination →   ┈┈▶ phytoremediation

ENVIRONMENTAL stability

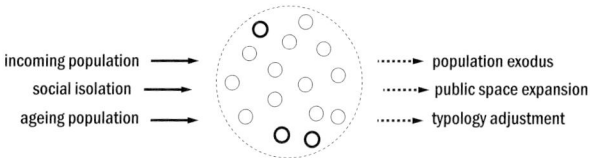

incoming population →   ┈┈▶ population exodus
social isolation →   ┈┈▶ public space expansion
ageing population →   ┈┈▶ typology adjustment

social stability

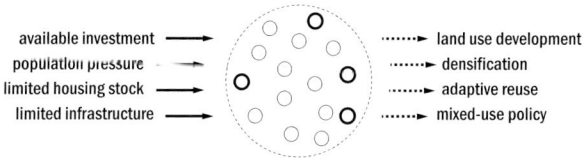

available investment →   ┈┈▶ land use development
population pressure →   ┈┈▶ densification
limited housing stock →   ┈┈▶ adaptive reuse
limited infrastructure →   ┈┈▶ mixed-use policy

economic stability

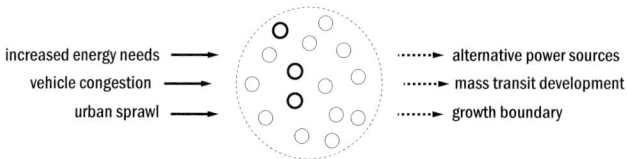

increased energy needs →   ┈┈▶ alternative power sources
vehicle congestion →   ┈┈▶ mass transit development
urban sprawl →   ┈┈▶ growth boundary

INFRASTRUCTURAL stability

TYPOLOGY

TYPOLOGY IS A SYSTEM OF CLASSIFICATION OF TYPES. A type is a pattern which becomes repeated because it has been shown to be successful (see *Pattern*). The pattern information that creates a type describes the fundamental characteristics of something. This defines its basic identity as an instance of a larger category. The information is based not on visual features but on organisational rules describing essential elements and relationships that must be present for the pattern to succeed. The typological pattern for a hammer, for example, is a striking surface and a grip. Every instance of a hammer has these two elements. However, once this pattern is satisfied, all other aspects of the hammer can vary. The material might be steel, wood, fibreglass, or rubber; the grip might be a long or short shaft; the weight and size might vary; and the head might have a second face with a flat striking surface, pick, claw, or ball. The variations are based on the need and context of use, while the typological pattern remains consistent. We understand every hammer to be part of a larger object classification that helps us to identify its nature and use. It also allows us to design new hammers by starting with its typological information.

Type and typology are standard classification tools found in many disciplines and applications in human thinking. An urban type refers specifically to the event-to-form relationship defining the composition of a space. *Event-to-form* means that the physical composition of that space is a reflection of the activities that occur in that space. At the urban scale, major activities relate to urban density, size, and arrangement of buildings and their lots (see *Grain*); the intensity and efficiency of activities on land, and types of uses supported by buildings and open space (see *Use*); the configuration of movement infrastructure (see *Path* and *Permeability*); and the relationship of roads to urban objects and spaces (see *Mobility*

DOI: 10.4324/9781003254935-53

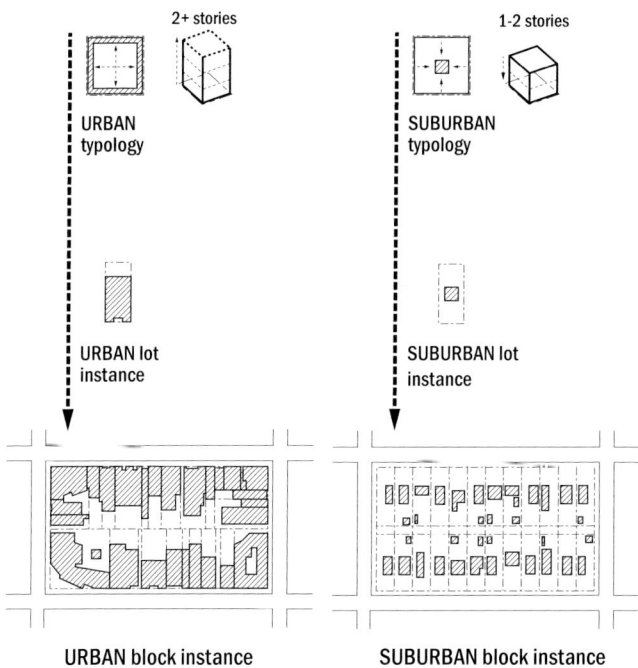

2+ stories

URBAN typology

URBAN lot instance

URBAN block instance

1-2 stories

SUBURBAN typology

SUBURBAN lot instance

SUBURBAN block instance

and *Figure-Ground*). Typology always uses physical characteristics and relationships as a compositional pattern to refer to socio-cultural events and human interactions.

Urban design uses typological patterns in building massing, street, and block layout, as well as infrastructure and land use configurations to understand spatial organisation and their social impacts (see *Typo-Morphology*). For each, there is always an essential formal relationship governing the type in the same way as in the hammer example. As a typology, that relationship is necessarily present, but all other aspects of the instance can vary based on local context, such as topography, culture, climate, and resources. For example, if we consider the difference between suburban and urban areas, we could describe it in one of several different ways, such as density of population, access to natural elements, street corner conditions, or the style of housing. Each of these aspects provides a different description based on variation in context. However, the typological information defines the formal relationship, which is fundamental and present in all instances of urban or suburban form. The essential difference between these two areas is the mass-to-property-line relationship. Urban typology aligns the major building mass to the property edge. Suburban typology pulls the major building mass away from the exterior property line. This difference in formal configuration manifests differences in social values and economic priorities of principles like privacy and exposure in relation to street frontage.

Within urban complexity, typology offers tools for sustainability through the implementation of successful patterns. It also helps to develop and maintain a specific identity of communities through continuity and stability of urban elements.

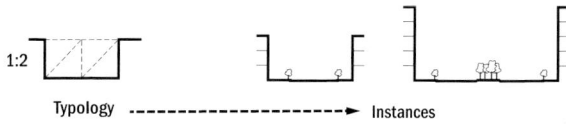

1:2

Typology ---------------------------> Instances

STREET typologies

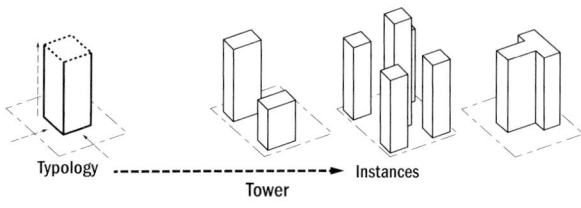

Typology ---------------------------> Instances

Tower

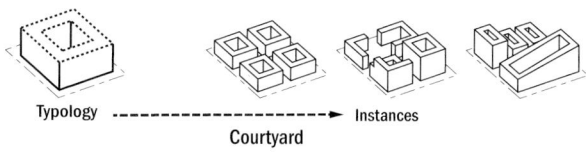

Typology ---------------------------> Instances

Courtyard

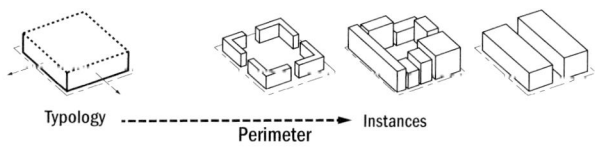

Typology ---------------------------> Instances

Perimeter

BLOCK typologies

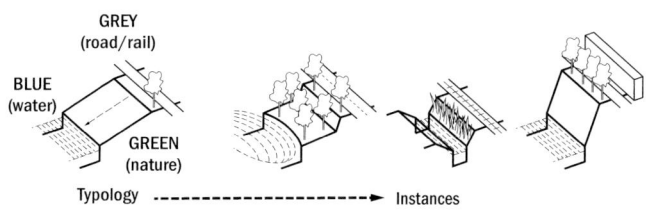

GREY
(road/rail)

BLUE
(water)

GREEN
(nature)

Typology ---------------------------> Instances

INFRASTRUCTURE typologies

USE

A USE IS AN ACTIVITY ALIGNED WITH a purpose or employed to achieve an outcome. We generally understand use through how we engage or take hold of an object to do something. When that object fits our needs or performs an act beneficial to us, we consider it *usable*. There is often a sense of consumption to the idea of use. People understand, through use, that things are finite, and once they have achieved their purpose, they might no longer be what they once were. We apply the idea of use to everything around us, from objects to spaces and even other people. As we engage objects and spaces, we determine what they can do for us and use this as a way to define their identity.

In urban design, use refers to the activities and events associated with occupation that are supported through allowing or restricting specific built form, open space, infrastructure, and activities. These events are grouped together into larger categories to apply a characteristic or identity to an area (see *Containment* and *Identity*). The term that is applied to this particular application of use is *land use*. As urban form supports the activities of people, the way we expect a space to be used is reflected in urban massing, grain patterns, infrastructure patterns, and proximity (see *Grain*, *Pattern*, and *MATBH: Proximity*). For example, commercial land use in urban settings is typically along the street edge to provide easy visibility and access. Residential land use, in contrast, is located away from the street for the same reason—to reduce visibility and provide privacy through reduced access. Urban grain can influence human experience and opportunities of interaction through how openings provide access from exterior to interior space. Use is manifested in the number, types, and distribution of openings which influences physical and visual accessibility.

Use can be based on the informal everyday practice of people as well as on formal political entities like local municipal codes and government

DOI: 10.4324/9781003254935-54

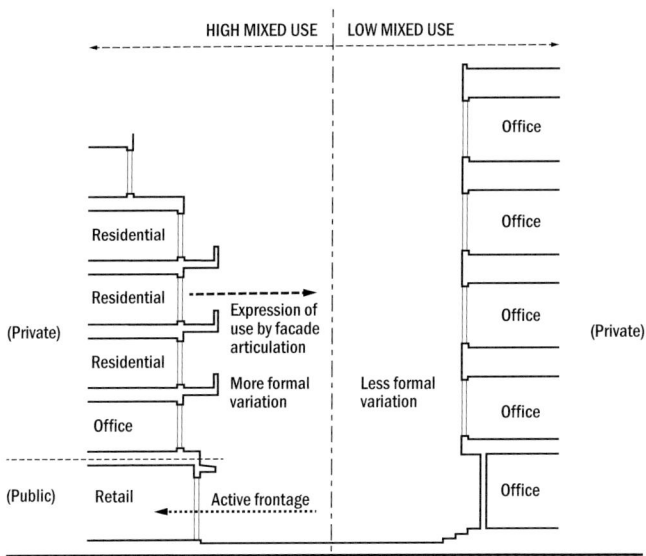

HIGH MIXED USE | LOW MIXED USE

Residential

Residential

Expression of use by facade articulation

Residential

More formal variation

Office

Retail

Active frontage

(Private)

(Public)

Office

Office

Office

Office

Office

Less formal variation

(Private)

INTEGRATION of use
BUILDING scale

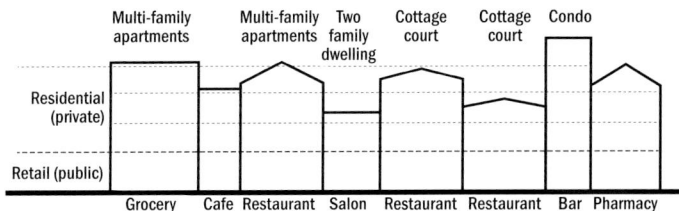

Multi-family apartments

Multi-family apartments

Two family dwelling

Cottage court

Cottage court

Condo

Residential (private)

Retail (public)

Grocery Cafe Restaurant Salon Restaurant Restaurant Bar Pharmacy

Variation within a SINGLE USE
STREET scale

policies. The notion of everyday use is evident at the scale of individual property and provides the smallest manifestation of urban activity in a space. These use patterns are often dynamic and change throughout the day, week, or year. Formal use is documented as broad categories and groups of events manifest in land use divisions through zoning regulations. Zoning use is a type of containment that divides the city into broad areas through legal regulations and codes. These are implemented to organise the city into manageable chunks and for coherence at the scale of neighbourhoods and districts. Different uses are categorised based on their relative compatibility captured in proximity with one another. The purpose is to increase positive interactions through adjacency of similar or compatible activities while avoiding negative interactions by excluding certain activities from the same area (see *Separation*). Separation of use through zoning is also deployed for environmental protection or human safety and security. The intention is efficient and effective organisation of an urban area without conflict.

Uses can be integrated, inclusive, excluded, or separated through urban massing and movement infrastructure. Integrated and inclusive uses are employed to create a mix of uses. An area with a mix and diverse set of uses enhances urban compactness, walkability, accessibility, and choice through diversity and proximity. Mixed use allows for spatial concentration of events and temporal continuity of activities, which can lead to an increase in publicness and stability through persistent sharing of resources and spaces.

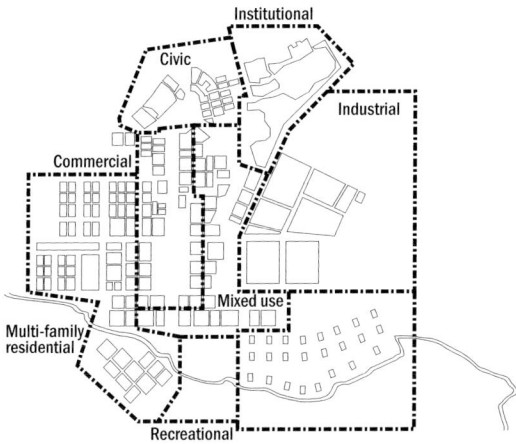

Land use as FUNCTIONAL ZONES

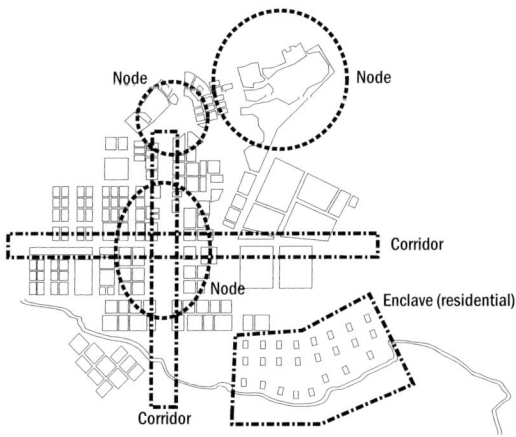

Land use as FORMAL ZONES

SOCIALLY CONSTRUCTED AGREEMENTS

DOI: 10.4324/9781003254935-55

THE WAY WE UNDERSTAND OURSELVES, other people, and our world is based on the layering of different sources of information. Our most basic knowledge is sensori-motor, which is the information experienced by our body through our senses. Seeing, hearing, smelling, tasting, touching, and feeling are all sources of this information. We also have environmental information, which is the knowledge of things outside of our bodies, such as sun, weather, sky, and ground. Our sensori-motor knowledge is situated with our environmental knowledge in a complex but fundamental relationship. We use this relationship to understand social information that is the shared knowledge of humans in physical relation to other humans. Where our body is located in space, its directionality, proximity, and visibility to others affects how we understand our relationships and opportunities. The previous sections of this book addressed these layers of knowledge.

This final section addresses more complex construction of meaning through social interaction and cultural interpretations. This is socio-cultural knowledge rooted in beliefs and behaviours using values, priorities, rules, interpretations, memories, and agreements among people. It is still based on embodied thinking, as how we inhabit the world is the basis of how we understand a shared experience with other people. However, this knowledge rests on agreements between people focused on their priorities and values, which can be contested or even conflictual between social groups. As shared knowledge, socially constructed agreements shape human occupation and action through maintaining a set of values as a foundation of habitation and development of our cities.

AUTHENTICITY

AUTHENTICITY IS A QUALITY THAT IS EXPERIENCED when a thing or event is determined to have all parts of its existence in alignment (see *Coherence*). It is a judgement, as people decide if something is authentic or not by interpreting the reliability of that thing's presence with its origin, materiality, form, and performance. As such, authenticity is connected to the human concept of truth. In urban design, authenticity is based on the alignment between the human experience of occupying a space and the formal characteristics of that space. Formal characteristics include material, shape and surface qualities, workmanship and construction techniques, and arrangement of parts and whole.

Authenticity can be understood through the presence of historical traces of objects in our environments, relating development history, past events, and cultural memory of a location (see *Locality*). Historic authenticity is based on the connection between how specific human experiences and shared social events are preserved through the form of our built environment. We find traces of our histories and past cultures in tangible elements of urban space like materials, objects, buildings, and structures, and spatial plans such as street layout, lot configurations, and built form massing (see *Typology* and *Typo-Morphology*). These fragments embody intangible elements like traditions, memories, rituals, and histories. When we, as a culture or community, decide which fragments to preserve and which to remove, we are using the built environment to express our values. In these discussions of urban conservation, authenticity is commonly used in the definition and evaluation of heritage of a place.

Alternatively, authenticity is a judgement found as a contemporary idea. This form of authenticity occurs when space in urban environments expresses the fullness of a lived experience of human habitation (see *Character* and *Place*). It includes how diverse human occupation, activities,

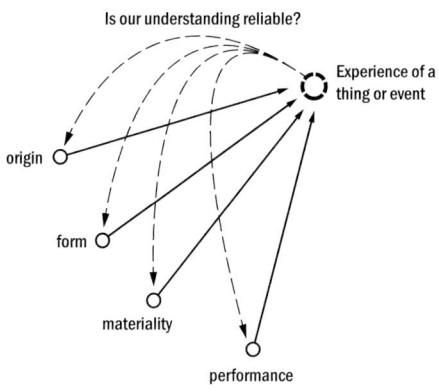

Is our understanding reliable?

origin

form

materiality

performance

Experience of a
thing or event

Authenticity through RELIABILITY

rituals, and traditions are integrated through physical characteristics, spatial plan, and material expression of a space. For example, in an active urban area such as an entertainment district, positive human experiences occur based on spatial characteristics and are supported through urban notions of alignment, activated edges, enclosure, and publicness. The space might be enjoyable for a few hours as a visitor but is not an authentic experience, as the arrangement of space and activities are focused on a very narrow aspect of human experience. For this district to be *authentic*, spatial attributes should express broader aspects of the lived space, including habitation patterns, a rich quality of life for everyone including residents and workers, and a widening of possible activities. This might include more diverse commercial patterns extending to grocery stores and other daily needs, as well as institutional and recreational support for families with schools and recreational opportunities. Contemporary authenticity requires a multi-dimensional alignment between everyday human activities and the arrangement of the physical environment.

Since authenticity is a human judgement based on interpretation of a place, we might not all agree which historic time period, which structures, or whose needs represent the true identity of a locality to enable a genuine lived experience. We should examine what an authentic urban environment might be within the context of diverse groups of people holding different values and supporting different actions and spaces (see *Diversity*). As communities evolve, the answer to these questions will affect the formal composition of our contemporary urban spaces. As such, authenticity is an important idea that engenders discussion and reflection, evaluating our values through the physical environment. Authenticity affects choice through decisions of preservation, renewal, and alteration in communities.

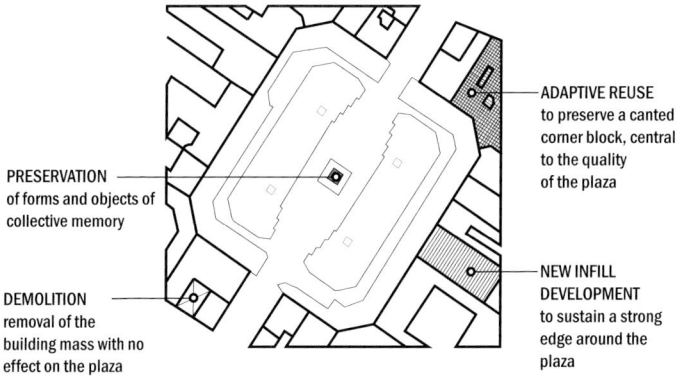

PRESERVATION
of forms and objects of
collective memory

ADAPTIVE REUSE
to preserve a canted
corner block, central
to the quality
of the plaza

DEMOLITION
removal of the
building mass with no
effect on the plaza

NEW INFILL
DEVELOPMENT
to sustain a strong
edge around the
plaza

HISTORIC AUTHENTICITY
Value of past fragments and its continuity

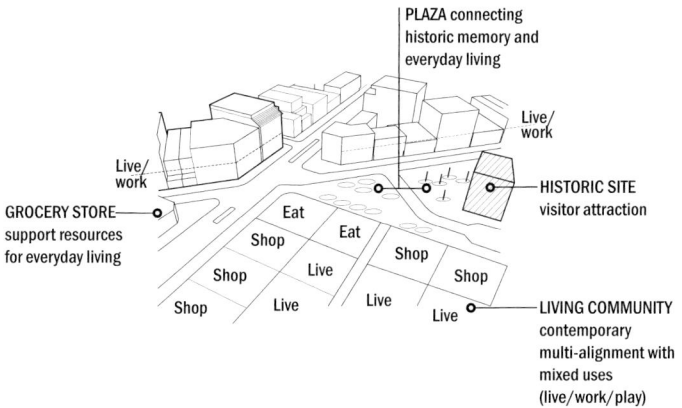

PLAZA connecting
historic memory and
everyday living

Live/
work

Live/
work

GROCERY STORE
support resources
for everyday living

HISTORIC SITE
visitor attraction

Eat

Shop

Eat

Shop

Shop

Live

Shop

Shop

Live

Live

Live

Live

LIVING COMMUNITY
contemporary
multi-alignment with
mixed uses
(live/work/play)

CONTEMPORARY AUTHENTICITY
Value of broad and persistent lived experiences

CHARACTER

CHARACTER IS THE DISTINGUISHING FEATURE that makes one thing different from another. When referring to people, we use the term *character* to refer to the fundamental beliefs and moral choices that define a person. When we consider the character of something that is not human, we base our interpretation by projecting human values onto non-human things (see *MATBH: Personification*). If the thing is capable of action, such as an animal, we interpret physical behaviour and activities to describe its temperament and demeanour. A family pet might be labelled with human concepts like caring, honest, trustworthy, or greedy. When something is not capable of action, such as an inanimate object, we use the term to interpret the physical features of a thing to represent human values and personalities.

In an urban context, character is the inherent collective sensory quality of a location. This quality makes the area distinct from others and produces interest (see *Locality*, *Interest*, and *Place*). Sensory quality includes all human experiences from sight and touch to smell and sound, while distinct means being recognisably different from other things. Urban character is based on the experience of physical form and infrastructure patterns such as building massing and grain, solid to void ratios, materiality, natural elements, and movement configuration (see *Grain*, *Connectedness*, *Landmark*, *Rhyme*, *Rhythm*, and *Locality*). Distinctness is often expressed through local vernacular characters based on traditions of building, material access, craft, detailing, and construction in specific locations. We might find a particular, locally available building material, such as a stone or brick, used amongst many buildings to create a distinct character. Urban archaeological traces, such as old city walls, pre-industrial canals, or historic buildings, can produce distinct character. Environmental qualities such as weather patterns, elevation, air quality, topography, and light quality also combine

DOI: 10.4324/9781003254935-57

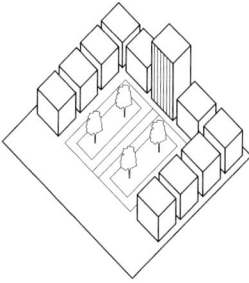

FORMAL and FOCUSED

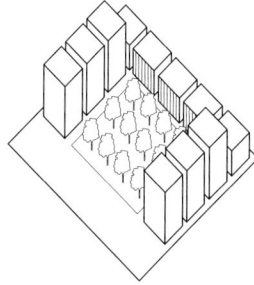

FORMAL and GENERAL

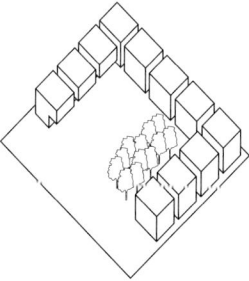

INFORMAL and FOCUSED

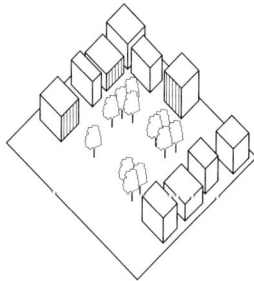

INFORMAL and GENERAL

Character through PHYSICAL COMPOSITION and QUALITIES

with built forms to create distinctness in an area, especially when those qualities affect the arrangement and experience of urban space (see *MATBH: Force*). Building organisation in hot, dry climates might favour tall, narrow streets to minimise solar exposure in public areas, while more moderate climates support wider and more open public spaces to allow interaction and experience under the sun. Each of these patterns produces a different urban character.

Socio-cultural activities and historic associations unique to a locality can affect our interpretation of urban character. This involves the current and past use of spaces. These expressions of character can manifest through the qualities of public gathering spaces based on unique events localised to an ethnic or cultural group. In these cases, the urban space is shaped by the particular ritual or social needs of the events. For example, a festival or a demonstration occurs in streets and plazas because such public spaces allow space for ritualised street performances or large gatherings. The publicness is manifest in physical characteristics offering flexibility in adapting to temporary changes in accessibility patterns. Similarly, a market with a specific bargaining culture is expressed in the physical layout of retail stalls, centrality of the auction halls, and rhythm of use patterns and movement patterns. Memorials or landmarks can also create spatial distinctness through memory and significance of public spaces as locations for important cultural events.

Urban character can change over time, and the physical expression of character is often tied to issues of authenticity, place identity, and attachment (see *Authenticity* and *Identity*). While character is based on physical expression, it is often interpreted by people as a feeling, general atmosphere, and ambience of a place.

Public spaces with same formal dimensions but
different event adjacency create different character
1. Formal civic square
2. Public park/recreation area
3. Market square
4. Residential dog park

Ceremonial processional path

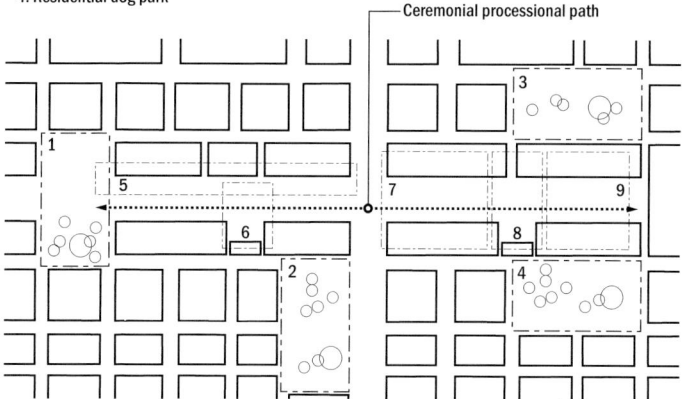

Same street changes character through social events
5. Street vendors
6. Playground
7. Sidewalk dining area
8. Public stage area/entertainment
9. Public demonstration area

Urban character and SOCIO-CULTURAL RITUAL

CHOICE

CHOICE IS A TYPE OF AGENCY in which people have the opportunity of selecting one course of action from various available options. The act of choice allows us, as humans, to be agents in the world through analysing different options to achieve the same goal, regardless of whether that goal is conscious or unconscious. Where control is the agency to affect things around us, choice is the agency to resist the control of others (see *Control*). This individual notion of choice is central to human privacy as a condition to control one's own body and bodily actions like stasis, movement, orientation, accessibility, and balance.

In urban design, choice is the availability of different options at multiple scales. These options could range from available paths for movement (see *Mobility*), different opportunities of visual interest and vista (see *Visibility*), various events and activities (see *Use*), diverse patterns of mobility, and options of transportation infrastructure (see *Permeability* and *Accessibility*). Choice can be found in the specific local quality of a space that characterises available connections and accessibility (see *Character* and *Identity*). Choice might be constrained to a location, such as a district node or a neighbourhood centre, or it might span a larger metropolitan area. In a local area, choice is the likelihood of an element or space to be available and used based on occupation, movement, and experience. At a community scale, choice is related to accessibility in terms of available opportunities to diverse groups of people. An example could be available choices for schools in a neighbourhood, or alternate options of housing offered within a district, due to how those uses are distributed in the urban space. Urban design policies and implementation often generates, controls, and protects certain choices through zoning codes or private covenants. These mandated policies allow or restrict certain types of uses, which has social and economic implications on choices for different demographic groups.

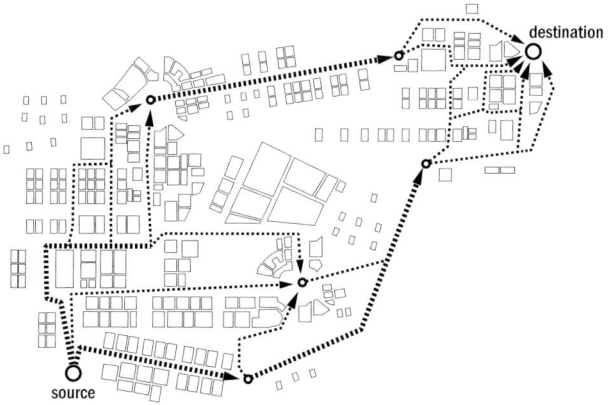

EXPERIENCE of choice through MOVEMENT

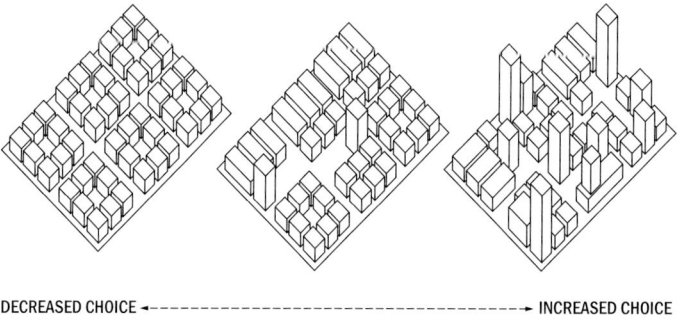

DECREASED CHOICE ◄- ► INCREASED CHOICE

Choice through DENSITY OPTIONS

For example, mandated single-family residential zones that prioritise large properties with minimum building size restrictions have a tendency to cater to higher income groups (see *Segregation*). On the other hand, when urban policies focus on integrating a wide range of different uses with various property sizes, types, densities, and mobility options, there are wider choice options for more diverse groups of people.

There are negative aspects of too much or socially unbalanced choice. At a physical environment level, too much choice can lead to lack of hierarchy and coherence, which decreases our ability to make sense of the environment (see *Legibility* and *Coherence*). At a socio-cultural level, choice implies that people have the ability to cause change in their environment through agency. Since our urban spaces are formed from a collection of communities, these changes have to be considered carefully and from several points of view. Communities are established and maintained through complex dynamic human relationships. The choices and actions of one person or community can have consequences for available choices for other individuals and groups. This social pressure of human-to-human relationships requires that we think about choice as an aspect of interactions with each other in a shared environment (see *Balance*). In this way, we should evaluate and balance options and alternative courses of action for different groups of people.

Alternative choices are important for urban sustainability and resilience. The available choices in density, mobility, use, destination, activity, and open spaces create greater flexibility and adaptability to changing situations and needs.

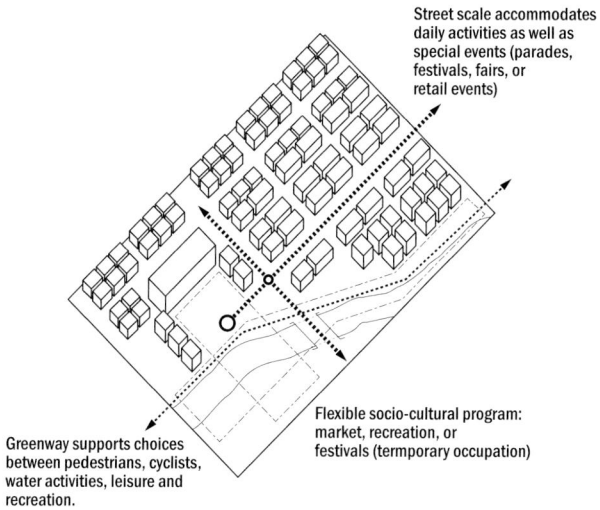

Street scale accommodates daily activities as well as special events (parades, festivals, fairs, or retail events)

Flexible socio-cultural program: market, recreation, or festivals (temporary occupation)

Greenway supports choices between pedestrians, cyclists, water activities, leisure and recreation.

Choice through ACCESSIBILITY

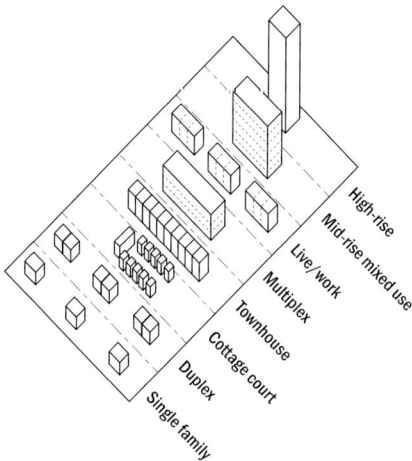

High-rise

Mid-rise mixed use

Live/work

Multiplex

Townhouse

Cottage court

Duplex

Single family

Choice through HOUSING FORM

DIVERSITY

DIVERSITY IS THE DEGREE OF variation recognised within a conceptual or physical area while still understanding them as part of a larger whole. Humans build relationships between things to make our understanding easier and faster (see *MATBH: Relationship*). While it is common to understand relationships through similarity, diversity allows us to understand relationships through difference. When we have a collection of things that do not seem to have an easily recognisable association or alignment, we can still create relationships and organise them through boundaries (see *Containment*), awareness (see *Presence*), or organising principles (see *Axis*, *Centre*, *Edge*, *Grid*, and *Node*). Perception of difference is based on our ability to understand plurality in our world. These concepts allow us to sort different things as a collection of mass or layers, as well as to manipulate them through adding, subtracting, separating, or merging of parts and whole.

In urban design, the concept of diversity can be understood through either forms or events. Formal diversity is the visual and compositional difference between physical elements in an environment. A diverse urban environment includes various lot and block sizing with a mix of grain patterns (see *Grain*). Building heights can vary in a range between low and high density. Age, material, and formal character support an urban area with many different building forms, surface textures, colour range, and physical expressions (see *Character*). Movement infrastructure is supported by a wide range of path types that allow for different forms of mobility including trails, sidewalks, mass transit, and vehicular circulation ranging from local roads to freeways (see *Grid* and *Mobility*). Event diversity is the presence of many different activities within proximity to each other in an environment (see *Use*). Event diversity can occur even in areas without formal diversity, but they often support each other through form-to-event patterns (see *Typology*).

DOI: 10.4324/9781003254935-59

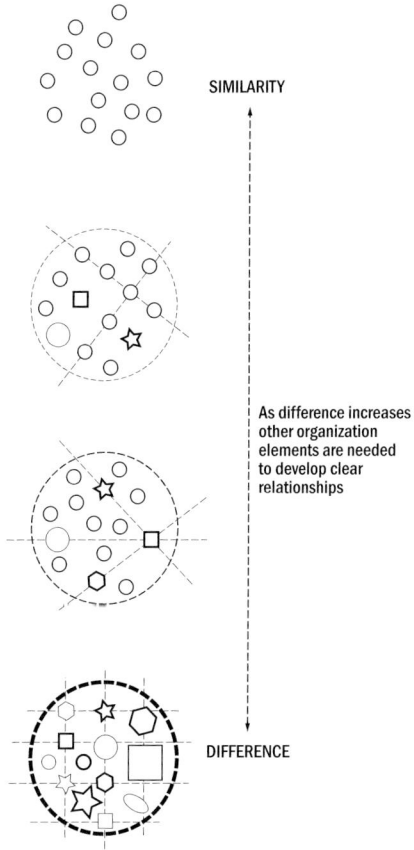

SIMILARITY

As difference increases
other organization
elements are needed
to develop clear
relationships

DIFFERENCE

Relationships through DIFFERENCE and SIMILARITY

Diversity offers different opportunities for occupation, interaction, and experience (see *Choice*). Both formal and event diversity are connected to our interpretation of more complex patterns in our surroundings, creating interest through difference (see *Pattern* and *Interest*). Diversity can create inclusive communities connecting variation in density and building types to different events and well-integrated movement infrastructure. As such, diversity becomes a tool to generate local identity with regional connections (see *Identity*). However, diverse areas, like neighbourhoods, can face challenges of accommodating resident groups with varied needs, tastes, and backgrounds reflected in their activities, uses of spaces, and patterns of interactions. Boundaries between adjacent spaces can become spaces of conflict; connectivity can clash with a need for security and privacy, and visual coherence can conflict with diverse tastes and styles.

Ultimately, diversity is about people and their beliefs, needs, and actions. While urban diversity is affected through physical composition and events, the purpose is to support social diversity and nurture human differences. The presence or absence of diversity in the built environment can indicate our socio-cultural beliefs through allowances, incentives, or restrictions. How we support, enable, or suppress activities of difference through ranges of spatial patterns of occupation and interaction reflect larger priorities (see *Control* and *Separation*). Diversity is an expression of balance as part of the longer-term health of urban environments. An attempt to balance multiple beliefs, needs, and activities through diverse urban forms and compositions is fundamental to sustaining healthy growth, development, and resilience in cities.

Increased socio-economic diversity through accessibility to mobility

Integrated area with diversity through adjacency

metro or lightrail

4

2

3

1

4

3

1

2

Urban area defined by socio-economic status
1. High income bracket
2. Medium income bracket
3. Low income bracket
4. Below poverty threshold

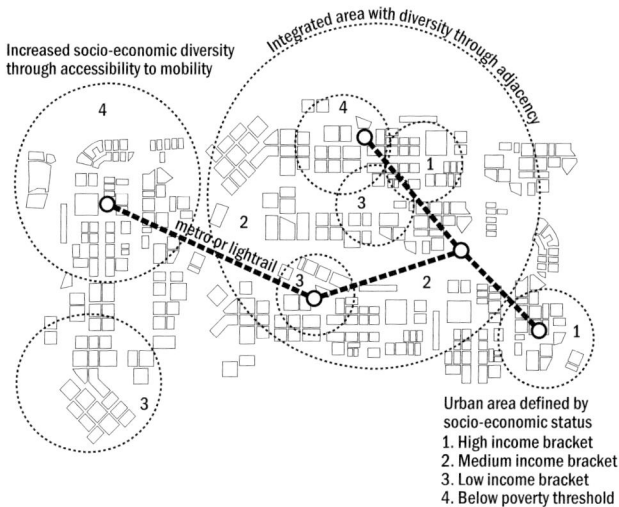

Diversity and CONNECTEDNESS

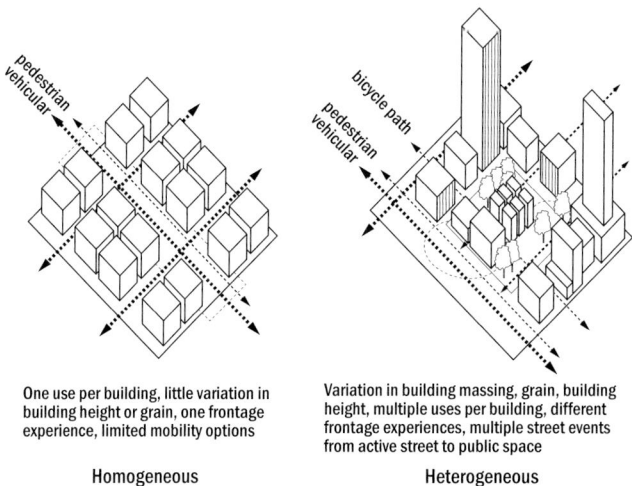

pedestrian
vehicular

bicycle path
pedestrian
vehicular

One use per building, little variation in building height or grain, one frontage experience, limited mobility options

Variation in building massing, grain, building height, multiple uses per building, different frontage experiences, multiple street events from active street to public space

Homogeneous

Heterogeneous

BALANCE through BLOCK Diversity

IDENTITY

IDENTITY IS WHO WE THINK WE ARE through how we relate ourselves to other entities that exist around us. Many factors make up an identity, including experiences, social interactions, belief systems, physical qualities, and abilities. The combination of all these aspects forms a whole, which defines an identity. While our own identity occurs inside our heads, we express that identity outwardly through our actions, life choices, treatment of others, and physical expressions of body stance, fashion, and the things we arrange around us (see *Character*). We think of identity as a point of difference between ourselves and everything around us, that which makes us distinct or unique. The only way we know a person who is not us is by interpreting their actions and physical characteristics through knowledge of our own values, traits, and expressions. Similarly, we project our personal human capacities, interests, and desires onto non-human things (see *MATBH: Personification*). We *know* something because we can relate its identity to something we understand about ourselves. Our sense of identification with something is an expression of similarity rather than difference.

Urban spaces do not have identities; people give them identities. While we interpret urban environments through embodied experience of the physical composition, it is understood through our identity using the sensory experience of our body. When we move through a commercial street or a housing development, we associate different types of sensory information from the environment together with our own experiences and cultural background to interpret our position and relationship to that space (see *Place*). Ask yourself why some might feel more comfortable in one housing form, such as a detached single family, rather than another, such as a multifamily condominium? How does one rather than the other suit you or align with your values of safety and security? How does it become an expression of your place of belonging? Identity is an evolving and

DOI: 10.4324/9781003254935-60

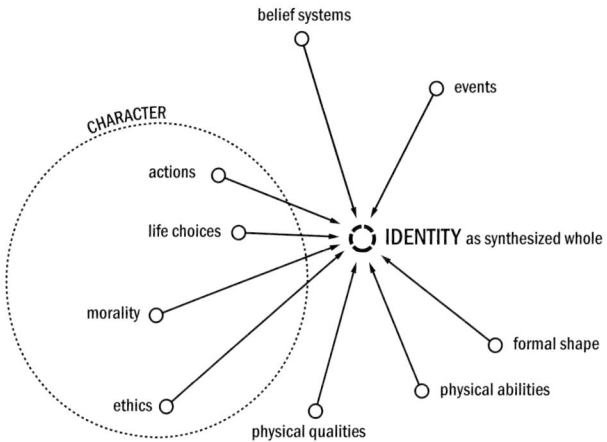

belief systems

events

CHARACTER

actions

life choices

IDENTITY as synthesized whole

morality

ethics

formal shape

physical abilities

physical qualities

Identity FORMATION and VALUES

dynamic concept rather than a fixed quality inherent in the physical nature of an urban space. It is based on our own values as an act of personal interpretation rather than something absolutely inherent to a thing. When people have different values, we can interpret the environment around us in different ways, essentially giving the same urban space different identities at the same time. This process of constructing and connecting with self, other people, and the surrounding environment through various identities is important for understanding and making places.

The identity of urban environments is interpreted through formal arrangement and physical attributes of objects in urban spaces. This also involves sensory and experiential information such as the events and social activities contained or supported by those spaces (see *Typology* and *Use*). While identity involves many small details, it is ultimately the expression of a whole. Urban identity extends across multiple scales from house (personal) and street to neighbourhood (social), district, city, and region (political). Each of these scales influences our understanding of the others, either through similarity or contrast. The character of a neighbourhood will influence our understanding of a street within that neighbourhood as well as its containing city. At the same time, the identity of a city will affect our interpretation of a street. As we move from body to region, our experiences increase in complexity with more interactions and greater choice among competing environments. Identity, as a part-to-whole relationship, allows us to make sense of complex environments with differences (see *Sensibility* and *Diversity*).

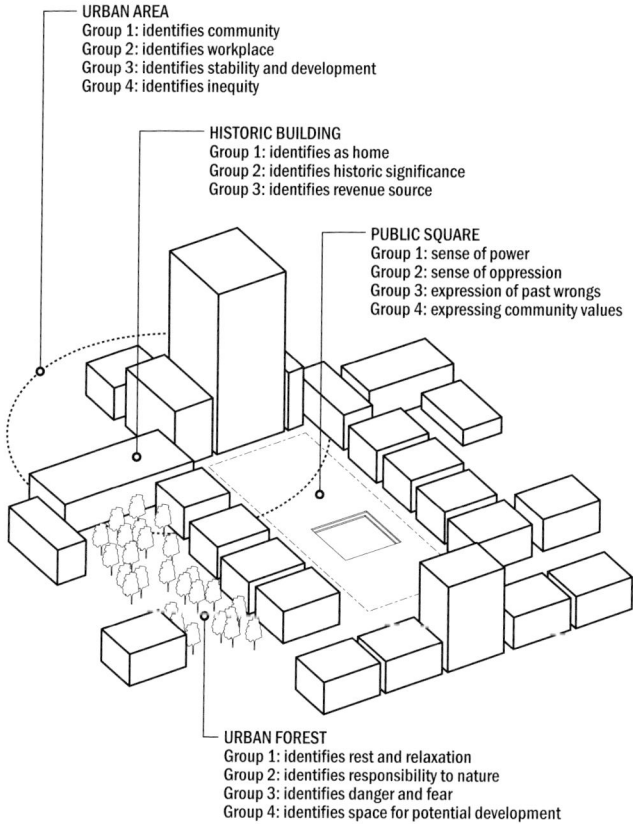

URBAN AREA
Group 1: identifies community
Group 2: identifies workplace
Group 3: identifies stability and development
Group 4: identifies inequity

HISTORIC BUILDING
Group 1: identifies as home
Group 2: identifies historic significance
Group 3: identifies revenue source

PUBLIC SQUARE
Group 1: sense of power
Group 2: sense of oppression
Group 3: expression of past wrongs
Group 4: expressing community values

URBAN FOREST
Group 1: identifies rest and relaxation
Group 2: identifies responsibility to nature
Group 3: identifies danger and fear
Group 4: identifies space for potential development

Same urban configuration creates several different identities
based on experiences of socio-cultural groups

Identity through CULTURAL PERSPECTIVE

INTEREST

INTEREST IS WHEN SOMETHING NOT ONLY draws our attention but generates a desire in us to engage with that thing, event, or situation. As we inhabit the world, we constantly organise information from surroundings through our senses. Instances of contrast, adjacency, axis, balance, repetition, spatial position, and centrality are associated into larger patterns which help us make sense of the world more quickly. In these moments, we look for hierarchical information to focus our attention on moments of relative importance (see *MATBH: Hierarchy*). Most of these interactions are passive, as we interact with entities like objects, buildings, spaces, and other people around them. However, interest occurs when the awareness of our attention shifts from passive recognition to active engagement. This moment generates curiosity and a desire to gain knowledge or enrich our lives through prioritising a preferred experience.

In the urban environment, interest starts with the awareness of an individual to the presence of events and physical elements that surround them (see *Presence*). This might be through an area prioritised by an ordering principle, such as the point where two axes cross or the centre of a circle. It might be through urban events when spaces are organised to have high and diverse activities (see *Activation*). It might also exist through a contrast that creates difference and then draws the attention of inhabitants (see *MATBH: Difference*). When we arrange the environment in a unique or unexpected way, which is still sensible and in support of the activities present, the potential for interest increases. This might be a surprising breaking of a grid organisational pattern, a change in grain and block patterns, or the overlay of several different mobility networks to make a complex infrastructural network. In all these cases, the shift from attention to interest is an act of gathering our attention to focus our awareness towards involvement.

DOI: 10.4324/9781003254935-61

Movement/view corridors provide access and choice

Difference through centrality, detail and scale, use and activity, solid-void contrast

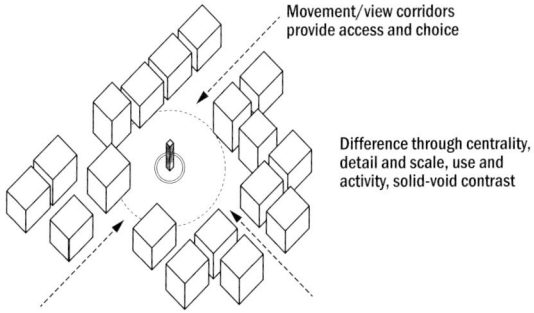

Interest through DIFFERENCE

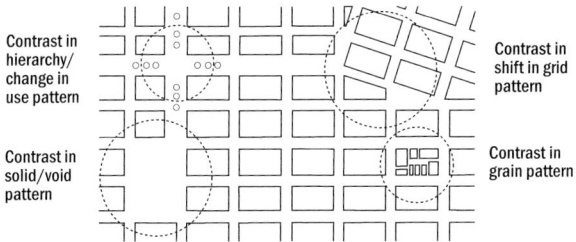

Contrast in hierarchy/ change in use pattern

Contrast in solid/void pattern

Contrast in shift in grid pattern

Contrast in grain pattern

Interest through CONTRAST IN PATTERN

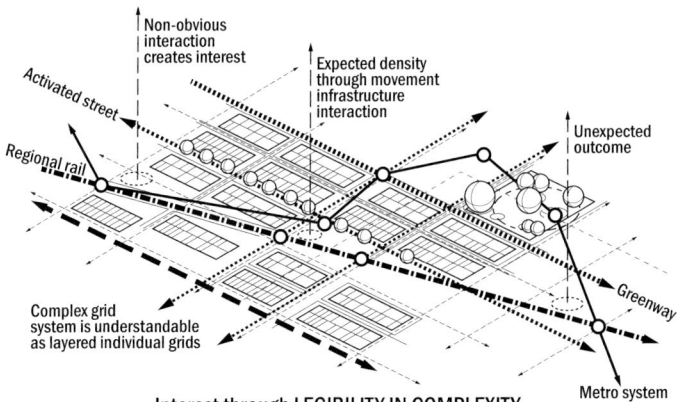

Non-obvious interaction creates interest

Expected density through movement infrastructure interaction

Activated street

Regional rail

Unexpected outcome

Complex grid system is understandable as layered individual grids

Greenway

Metro system

Interest through LEGIBILITY IN COMPLEXITY

Interest can also be generated by mystery as found in degrees of complexity, difference, and legibility. Mystery generates interest through the possibility of unexpected or new experiences or implying future satisfaction by resolving incomplete information. In an urban environment, this can be achieved through combining an easily sensible location with intentional gaps in information or forms that are suggested by other elements but are not immediately perceivable. The partial glimpse of a larger pattern, the suggestion of a space hidden from our current view, and the slow revealing of a vista are all moments of incomplete environmental information, which can be linked to interest through mystery. One of the most important factors in mystery is the balance between making something easily understandable and creating complex environments that are experientially satisfying (see *Complexity*, *Legibility* and *Coherence*). While comprehension is important for our need for safety and security, environments that are too easy to understand offer too little stimulus to maintain our interest. Likewise, when our environment is too complex or confusing, we lack the ability to identify with it and also lose interest (see *Place*).

Interest in urban design is situational and focused around a particular situation, condition, or subject. Its effect can shift between social groups and cultural conditions. Also, differences can extend well past formal conditions and begin to address potential new experiences through the adjacency or integration of socio-cultural variation (see *Diversity*). The key is curating interest through a balance between coherence and difference as well as between complexity and legibility. Legibility reduces stress related to confusion, while interest enhances curiosity and continuous engagement—together supporting a rich urban experience.

Partial view of form or event creates interest through suggesting what might happen

Visible parts suggest other things that might be present

1. Path choice based on interest
2. Massing suggests public event
3. Glimpse of landmark
4. Unexpected urban-nature contrast
5. Minor change in pattern

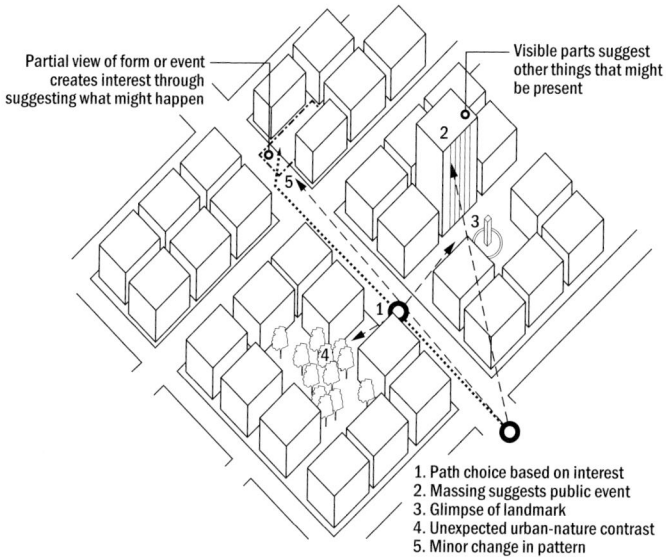

Mystery through FORESHADOWING

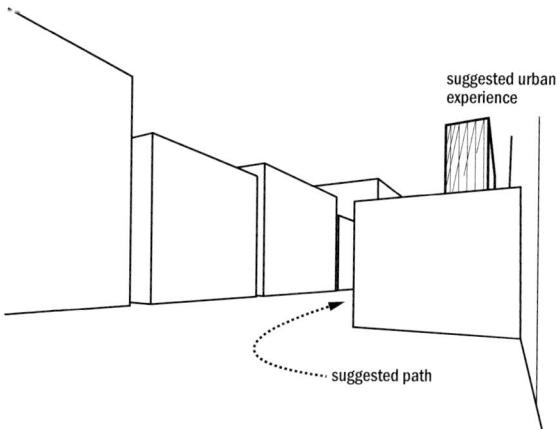

suggested urban experience

suggested path

Mystery through SUGGESTED PRESENCE

PLACE

PLACE IS A LOCALE WHOSE SENSE OF DISTINCTNESS is associated with the human capacities of belonging, engagement, and purpose. It involves the basic compositional qualities of space such as physical dimension and boundary as well as socio-temporal content related to position, orientation, exposure, and mobility of bodies (see *Locale* and *Space*). However, the idea of place layers our experience of space with additional socio-cultural associations such as identity operating through temporal knowledge of memory, prior experience, and recollection along with actions of involvement and preference (see *Control*, *Choice*, and *Interest*).

Humans construct a sense of place in the environment when we experience a bounded and situated space through both difference and similarity. Difference allows us to distinguish one area of space from another through characteristic features, disruptions in patterns, or moments of contrast (see *Character* and *MATBH: Difference*). It is through difference that we shift our general understanding of space into a specific locale. The larger the degree of distinctiveness of a location within its context, the stronger the possibility for interpretations of place to develop (see *Landmark*, *Rhyme*, *Rhythm*, and *Interest*). However, while one aspect of place is defined through difference, it also requires similarity to exist between the environment and the occupant. Similarity is a projection of our values to see a locale as an extension of ourselves (see *Identity*). We relate to that space in a way that builds a relationship through individual associations of belonging and identification. This includes how we evaluate and find alignment between our own values and the compositional elements in the locale, as well as past activities and connections with other people associated through memories in that locale. A place is a social agreement built through shared experiences with others, as well as an individual experience connected to memory attached to a specific location.

DOI: 10.4324/9781003254935-62

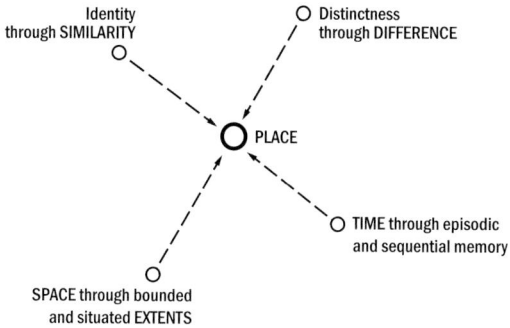

Place and EXPERIENCE

Our understanding of time is a factor that differentiates place from space. Time is impossible to separate from any human experience, but that sense of time can be sequential or episodic. As we occupy *space*, we engage a finite and bounded area with specific composition, scale, and arrangement of forms (see *Space*). This engagement is a direct experience that involves an understanding of time based on duration, or a linear series of connected moments of experience without interruption. However, as we construct a place identity, we experience both sequential time as well as episodic time. Episodic time recognises and links memories of past experiences and interactions at different times to enrich our current experience. The recollection of childhood associations, enjoyable interactions with friends, smells reminding us of past events, or the similarity to other favourite places can construct understanding and familiarity from long everyday use. These familiar personal recollections allow us to build a sense of security that associates our identity with that of a specific locale. A place experience embodies interactions, negotiations, and contestations toward a common cultural understanding, expressed in spatial control and access by different social groups. They become territories of collective memories, interpretations, and identities (see *Diversity*). Due to the balance between personal experience and cultural identity, a place is personal and, at the same time, worldly.

Place is not merely important in developing and maintaining identity. It also has a significant effect on human well-being and behaviour of stewardship. People are more involved when they feel they belong, including the tendency to participate in creating, changing, or maintaining their physical surroundings to reflect themselves through attachment to places.

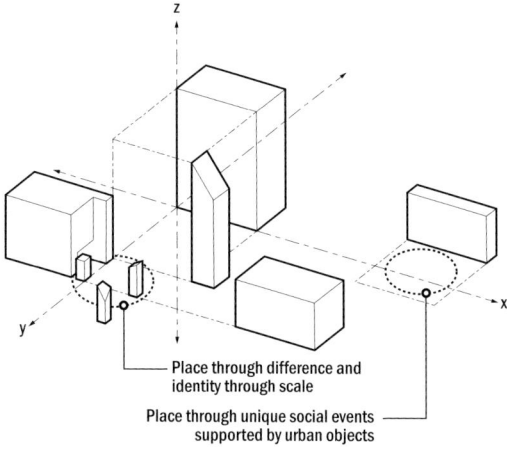

Place through difference and identity through scale

Place through unique social events supported by urban objects

Place, SCALE, BOUNDARY, and EVENTS

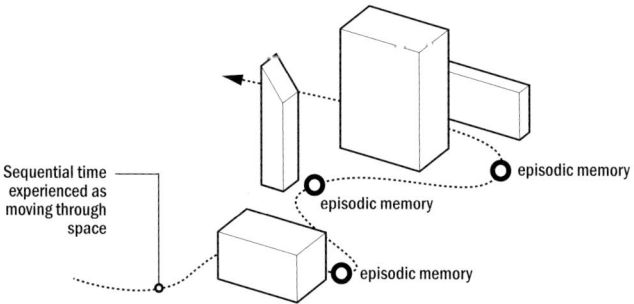

Sequential time experienced as moving through space

episodic memory

episodic memory

episodic memory

Place through TIME and MEMORY

SYMBOL

A SYMBOL IS SOMETHING THAT STANDS in for something else. It can be a physical object, mark, or event that represents something more abstract. Symbols are part of the human communication system, which help us understand the world we live in, bring meaning into our lives, and organise complex information (see *Complexity* and *MATBH: Metaphor*). We do this by using symbols to link parts of our environment to more abstract ideas that include human relationships, belief systems, and socio-cultural values. Rather than naturally occurring elements in our environment, symbols must be constructed and learned by an individual or group. Constructed meaning can be ambiguous, however, with the same symbol having different meanings for different people depending on their socio-cultural background, prior experiences, education, and upbringing (see *Diversity*).

Urban symbols occur in the relationship between people and the physical characteristics of elements in the built environment. These include the materiality, shape, arrangement, and patterns of urban spaces that become associated with something other than themselves through human agreement. For example, a civic building, such as a state capitol, might be a physical location where policy and legislative decisions are made, but it is also a cultural symbol that stands for who we are, or think we are, as a society.

Any aspect of the environment has the capacity to become a symbol should an individual or group assign meaning to it. However, spatial compositions that focus our attention have a higher likelihood of holding additional knowledge based on socio-cultural agreements. In this, urban hierarchy and organising principles of massing and movement infrastructure are important factors. Urban patterns such as distorted and hierarchical grids, centrality, radiosity, and nodes create the possibility for

DOI: 10.4324/9781003254935-63

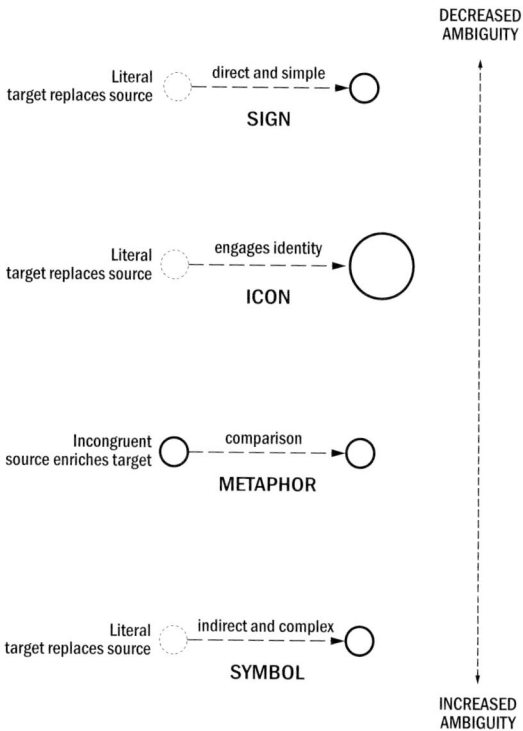

Meaning through ASSOCIATIONS

significance, heightened awareness, and interest (see *Node*, *Mobility*, and *Interest*).

Symbolic meaning occurs at multiple scales and through a wide variety of situations. These might be relatively small landmarks such as fountains, statues, and memorials, or larger ones such as public buildings and services (see *Landmark*). Open space in urban areas can take on symbolic meaning, ranging from shared gathering spaces of public squares to bounded natural areas such as urban forests. Physical locations in urban spaces acquire meaning through the events and rituals that take place in those spaces. These locations can be associated with types of gatherings, a dominant individual of power, religious rituals, community events, or personal memories associated with locations by residents. In all these situations, symbolic space becomes an important part of constructing our own identities and our sense of belonging with others in a community (see *Identity*). They are an aspect of how a space takes on a distinct character, holds an important memory, and expresses needs or services to construct a sense of place in our urban communities (see *Character* and *Place*). This does not mean that symbolic meaning is static or universal, as it exists as a shared agreement between people.

Symbols can provide vital connections between the past and the present in an urban environment as well as between different interpretations of people. In this way, some symbols may operate as urban icons. Icons are symbols codified by time and consistent use to have a simple and fixed meaning shared among many people. This is often a landmark with a distinctive outline, high presence, and differentiation used to create a brand identity for a city, district, or neighbourhood (see *Figure-Ground* and *Presence*). Symbols have an important role in the construction and sustenance of collective public memory.

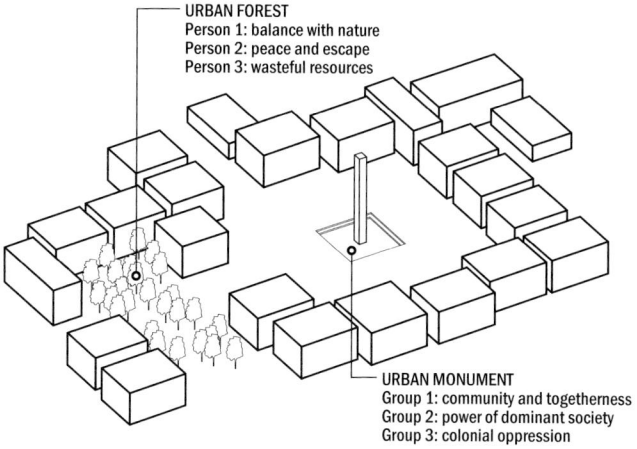

URBAN FOREST
Person 1: balance with nature
Person 2: peace and escape
Person 3: wasteful resources

URBAN MONUMENT
Group 1: community and togetherness
Group 2: power of dominant society
Group 3: colonial oppression

Symbol and AMBIGUITY

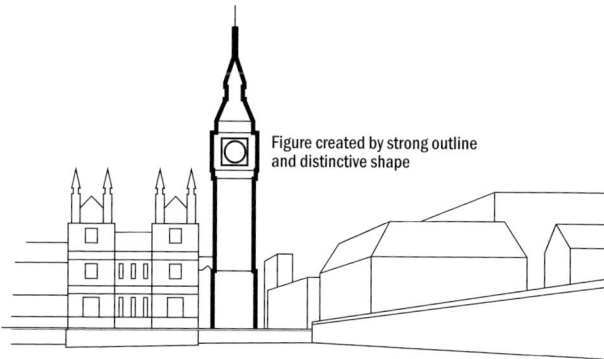

Figure created by strong outline
and distinctive shape

Symbol and ICON

TYPO-MORPHOLOGY

TYPO-MORPHOLOGY IS UNDERSTANDING THE evolution of an urban environment through the arrangement of physical elements focused on repeated patterns. The idea is based on combining two aspects of the built environment—morphology and typology. Morphology is the study of form and structure. When applied to urban design, morphology refers to understanding the city through the physical characteristics of the built environment and their arrangement to examine the formation and trans-formation of human settlements. This is generally focused on the urban grain formed by streets, open spaces like plazas and squares, sidewalks, and blocks in relation to vegetation and topography (see *Grain*). Typology is the study of types or fundamental, successful patterns repeated over time (see *Typology*). An urban type is the expression of a simple rule describing the physical relationship between elements, as reflective of specific human social occupation and activities. Typo-morphology, then, is considering the spatial organisation of urban environments through the formal configuration of what types are present, what social capacities they hold, and how they change over time.

A typo-morphological study involves documentation and analysis of three morphological types: street patterns, lot or plot patterns, and building patterns. Street patterns reveal the type and connection of movement infrastructure (see *Connectedness*, *Mobility*, *Permeability*, and *Accessibility*). They also provide the first level of organisation of the city into blocks using patterns of networks, axes, alignment, and rigidity (see *Grid*). The lot patterns within blocks depict how properties are arranged to reflect territorial control (see *Boundary*, *Block*, *Control*, and *Use*). The property boundary of the lot is a bounded area of legal ownership through which certain types of occupation are allowed or denied at a socio-political level. An individual can exercise control based on who has access

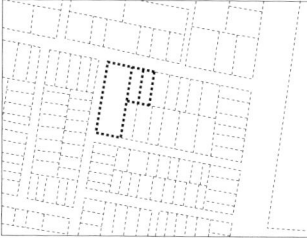

LOT/PLOT
Underlying pattern of
legal control through boundary

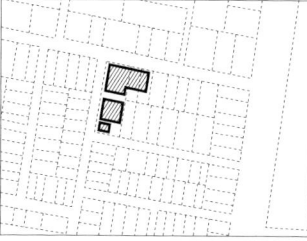

MASSING
Underlying pattern
defined by built form and use

BLOCK
Underlying pattern of
property boundaries

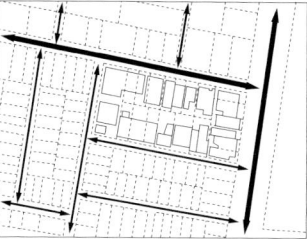

STREET
Underlying pattern of
mobility infrastructure

Typo-morphological ELEMENTS

and who can occupy, use, and affect the plot. These patterns of events, activities, and occupation influence composition of the built form through massing, frontage, materiality, and solid-void relationships (see *Density* and *Figure-Ground*).

Urban areas can be understood as socially constructed spaces reflecting human beliefs and actions of how we move, how we control territories, and how we occupy and use those territories through built form. These actions and beliefs of infrastructure development, land subdivision, and building construction change over time, and cities change their form accordingly. Typically, this occurs through subtle reorganisation, transformation, resistance, and erosion of existing and historical types and patterns in the natural evolution of cities. Sometimes, the transformation could be abrupt due to natural calamities like earthquakes or flooding, or human-made disasters like war. Typo-morphology is one way that we can understand the existing urban environment as a point in a longer evolutionary process to consider how the city might or should transform in the future.

Typo-morphology engages how the hierarchy of urban elements reflect common socio-cultural understanding in the formation and transformation of the city (see *Place*). Human-assigned meaning and values, embedded in the physical elements of the city, influence the possibility of certain choices through control of events and policies in bounded space (see *Boundary*). This typo-morphological information forms a structural knowledge of place through linking values, events, and physical characteristics. Typo-morphological studies recognise the successive and sustainable nature of urban form balancing structural permanence in the urban characteristics with dynamic socio-cultural experiences of construction and control influencing their change over time.

ORIGINS: location (~200 years)

FORT
Located on movement infrastructure (river/road)

VILLAGE
Density at movement and resource nexus

MARKET TOWN
Formally planned new settlement between population centres (fort/farms/villages)

FARMS
Rural farms (use) and farmsteads (massing) at the edge of the river

VILLAGE
Land division and property distribution based on river access

CONSOLIDATION: expansion by aggregation (~100 years)

FRINGE INACTIVITY
Loss of use in fort and surrounding farms

FRINGE NODE
Concentration of density and activity expressing pressures of development separate from the core

CORE
Consolidation of the core with grid axial expansion, mix of events and massing patterns

FRINGE USE
Industrial use replacing farming due to changing societal needs

FRINGE MOVEMENT
Street grid following the rhythm of the farms along the river

DEFORMATION: expansion by connection (present urban condition)

VARIATION
Variation in permeability to accommodate privacy needs and security

EROSION & RESISTANCE
Erosion of historic block pattern and persistence of the historic trail as a new gateway to the town

ADDITION
Deformed street grid to accommodate natural features

SUB-DIVISION
Land development outside the core due to pressures from increasing population density

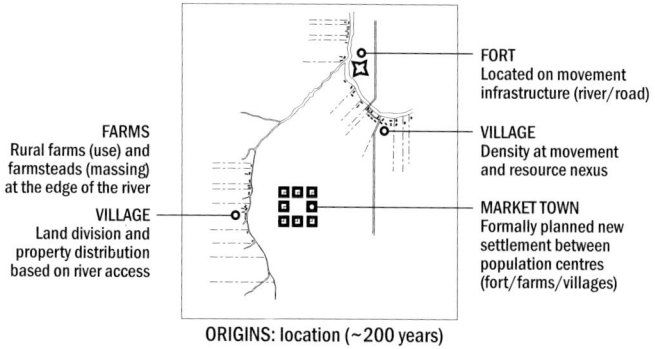

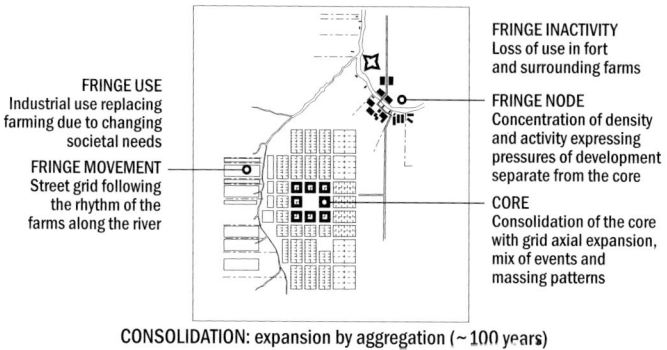

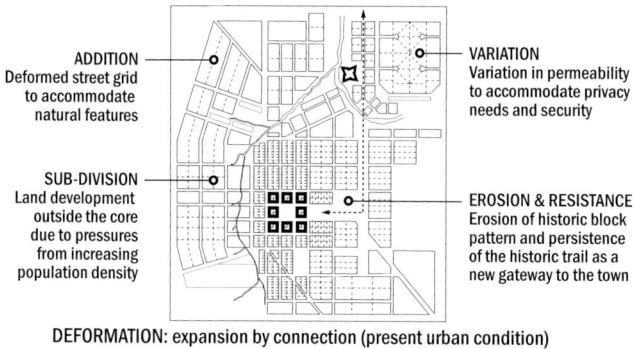

TRANSFORMATION of urban structure through two periods of EXPANSION

SOCIALLY CONSTRUCTED AGREEMENTS
TYPO-MORPHOLOGY

ABOUT THE AUTHORS

Anirban Adhya is Associate Professor of Architecture and Urban Design at Lawrence Technological University, USA. He focuses on highlighting underlying dimensions of architecture in the city that connects urban ecology, spatial typology, and everyday urbanism. His previous book, *Shrinking Cities and First Suburbs: The Case of Detroit and Warren, Michigan* (Palgrave, 2017) illustrated the ecology of problems and responses in metro Detroit. He has also written on evolving notions of publicness in *The Public Realm as a Place of Everyday Urbanism* (University of Michigan Press, 2008), and worked with communities in Buffalo, New York; Warren, Michigan; Seattle, Washington; and Monteverde, Costa Rica.

Philip D. Plowright is Professor of Architecture and Design Theory at Lawrence Technological University, USA. His interest focuses on developing clarity around foundational knowledge in the applied design disciplines for use in teaching and production environments. His previous book, *Making Architecture by Being Human* (Routledge, 2020), presented the cognitive building blocks of spatial semantics between individuals and spaces in relation to architectural values. He has also explored cognitive methodology in *Revealing Architectural Design* (Routledge, 2014), and embodied meaning in *Qualitative Embodiment in English Architectural Discourse* (Universidad de Castilla-La Mancha, 2017).